New Mexico
Cook Book

by

Lynn Nusom

**GOLDEN
WEST** ✺
PUBLISHERS

Cover Photo by Dick Dietrich

Library of Congress Cataloging-in-Publication Data

Nusom, Lynn.
  New Mexico cook book / by Lynn Nusom.

  Includes index.
  1. Cookery, American—Southwestern style. 2. Cookery—New
Mexico. I. Title
TX715.2S69N87   1990   641.59789—dc20   90-3391
ISBN 0-914846-48-5   CIP

Printed in the United States of America

7th printing, 1994   ˙

Information in this book is deemed to be authentic and accurate by
authors and publisher. However, they disclaim any liability incurred in
connection with the use of information appearing in this book.

Golden West Publishers   **(602) 265-4392**
4113 N. Longview Ave.
Phoenix, AZ 85014, USA

*Golden West Publishers books are available at special discounts to
schools, clubs, organizations and businesses for use as fund-
raisers, premiums and special promotions.
Send inquiry to Director of Marketing.*

Need a fund-raiser?
We can produce a book like this for your organization or club!
For more information contact:
"The Book Studio," c/o Golden West Publishers
4113 N. Longview, Phoenix, AZ 85014, (602) 274-6821

Dedication

To my wife, Guylyn Morris Nusom,
who introduced me
to New Mexican cooking!

Acknowledgement

Special thanks to the many
New Mexicans who have
generously shared
their recipes with me.

Contents

Introduction

New Mexico *is* the Land of Enchantment. Not only is this a Chamber of Commerce slogan and the state motto but most New Mexicans truly feel this way about their state.

In many American minds the boundaries of Mexico and New Mexico are blurred. In the late fifties I know of at least one case where an immigration official hassled the occupants of a car with New Mexico license plates as they tried to re-enter the country from Canada. Even as late as five years ago a friend of my mother's, in New York, told me how lucky I must feel having learned Spanish now that I was living in Mexico.

"New Mexico," I said.

"I know!" was her reply.

Many residents of New Mexico are indeed Mexican-Americans and many of the citizens are Spanish-American descendants from the original Spanish conquerors and settlers.

Too often overlooked, however, is the fact that there are a great number of people living in New Mexico with other cultural backgrounds. A great many Jewish families fleeing Russia, Germany, and other places that were intolerant of them at the time, migrated through Mexico to settle in New Mexico. In addition, there are Germans, Hungarians, Poles, the Irish, Swedes, etc., etc. The list is as never-ending and as varied as America itself.

There is a difference, however. There are many theories as to what causes this difference: climate, wide-open spaces, rugged terrain, imposing mountains, Spanish and Mexican influence, clear blue skies, the struggle for water, the quiet, some left-over unknown Indian soul wandering freely amongst us. Many things contribute to this feeling of difference and being special.

Whether native or transplanted, New Mexicans are fiercely loyal to their state and are understandably upset when a prominent newscaster mispronounces the names of their towns and cities on national television, or a New Jersey toll keeper jokingly wants to see their passports.

Just as the image of New Mexico is often blurred in the minds of others, so is the concept of what New Mexicans have eaten over the years. Just as New Mexicans are as varied a people as one will find anywhere, so is their food.

A great deal of the "native" cuisine in the state is Mexican, Spanish and Indian oriented. However, what is unique to one area, will often be prepared differently and taste different in various parts of the state, although the dish may bear the same name.

Most residents of the state when discussing their food preferences and what they really like, give chile great prominence. You'll note that in New Mexico chile has a habit of sneaking into recipes that normally would not call for it.

It is hard to find a group of people quite as rabid about one certain food as a New Mexican can be about chile. This may seem very strange to a Bostonian, but many a New Mexican, indeed, would feel that his whole being might just wither away if deprived of his chile.

Many a relative dutifully prepares care-packages of chile to send to displaced New Mexicans throughout the world.

So a New Mexican arriving back in his home state after an absence of even a few days wants to head for the nearest purveyor of chile.

Oh, the number of New Mexican romances that have started over a bowl of chile. Oh, the number of souls that have laid claim to having been saved by the same and there are even those who have professed to have cured their ulcers by massive doses of the stuff.

To be sure, an area reflects itself in the food that its citizens eat. A popular cliche some time back was "you are what you eat." If this is true, then New Mexicans eat some of the best food in the world as they certainly are some of the finest people in the world.

When autographing my cookbooks, I often write "Happy Cooking..." This is a very special phrase for me and I think that there is no better place to practice happy cooking than in New Mexico.

Lynn Nusom

CHAPTER ONE

The Indian Heritage in New Mexico Cooking

The Indian influence is very strong in New Mexico, as well it might be. After all, they were the first inhabitants. Unlike other areas of the country where the Indian legacy was snuffed out along with the bulk of the various tribes, in New Mexico it remains strong and, we hope, enduring.

There were several distinct groups of Indians in the state. The Apaches, mostly nomadic and warlike, lived from the hunt and on nuts and berries. The Plains Indians, such as the Comanches and the Utes, combined some of the aspects of Apache lifestyle with herd raising and a little crop cultivation.

Another group is the Pueblo Indians who got their name from their dwellings, or Pueblos, which were the forerunners of the modern apartment complex. These were many-storied buildings with "apartments" or rooms for the residents and communal rooms and spaces that included cooking areas and ovens.

The Pueblo Indians cultivated such crops as corn, squash, peanuts, beans and potatoes. Corn was one of the mainstays of the Indian diet, and they devised numerous ways to fix it.

Some of the Indian foods were made for ceremonial purposes. For example, a corn cake is still served in the Navajo celebration of the advent of puberty. Many recipes such as this one were made in accordance with the instructions from the deity Changing Woman.

The combination of their old ways, their gods and religious practices with those of Christianity is unique and often confusing to an outsider. It is the same with the language mixture. It can be a shock for a tourist to watch an Indian tribal dance such as the one at Tortugas during the Christmas festivities and then hear all the "Indians" speaking Spanish to one another.

Intermarriages between Spaniards, who first opened up New Mexico, and Indians is responsible not only for the bilingual and trilingual abilities of many New Mexicans, but also for many other local customs.

The foodstuffs also became intermingled and chile met corn, pork met squash, and lard was introduced. The Indians became both teachers and students. The result is a traditional cuisine that, although different from that of the rest of the world, is very, very tasty indeed.

The recipes in this chapter have been adapted for modern kitchens.

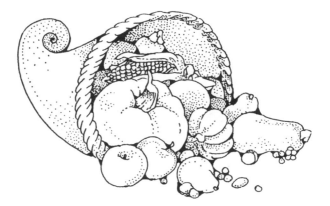

Corn Fritters

To a Pueblo Indian corn was the most important part of his diet. The corn was used fresh but more often dried and then ground into flour to make tortillas, bread, cakes and puddings.

The Spanish introduced lard and frying became popular. One way of preparing fresh corn was to cut it off the cob and fry it. The pioneer women adapted this method to various dishes. One of these was corn fritters. This recipe uses canned corn, but the same amount of fresh corn may be substituted.

1 EGG
½ cup MILK
1 Tbsp. LARD (or vegetable SHORTENING)
1 can (10 oz.) whole kernel CORN

1 tsp. BAKING POWDER
½ tsp. SALT
¼ tsp. ground BLACK PEPPER
LARD or vegetable SHORTENING for deep frying

Melt the tablespoon of shortening and beat the egg and milk into it. Add the corn and the rest of the ingredients and stir until mixed thoroughly.

Drop the mixture, a tablespoon at a time, into the hot fat and fry for four to five minutes or until brown. Drain on paper towels and serve hot. Makes 12 to 16 fritters.

Blue Corn Tortillas

2 cups BLUE CORN MEAL
1 cup BOILING WATER

Add as much of the cup of water to the blue corn meal as you need to make a medium-hard dough. Shape the dough into two-inch balls. Roll each ball out until it is very thin and cook on a lightly greased pancake griddle.

Makes approximately two dozen tortillas.

Navajo Corn Chowder

4 slices SALT PORK
(or very fat BACON)
1 med.-size yellow ONION
2 med.-size TURNIPS
2½ cups CHICKEN STOCK
(or canned CHICKEN
BROTH)
2 cups fresh CORN,
cut off the cob

4 Tbsp. all-purpose FLOUR
½ cup COLD WATER
2 cups MILK
1 tsp. PAPRIKA
1 tsp. GARLIC SALT
½ tsp. DRIED PARSLEY
2 oz. DRY SHERRY

Blanch the salt pork in enough water to cover in a deep skillet or pan, over low heat, for 10 minutes. Drain off the water and fry the salt pork over low heat until crisp. Remove from pan, and reserve. Peel, dice and add the onions to the pan and cook until golden brown. Peel turnips and cut into bite-sized pieces, stir into the onion, break up the salt pork into small pieces and return to the pan. Pour chicken stock over mixture in the pan, cover and simmer over medium heat for 20 minutes. Then stir in the corn.

In a mixing bowl, stir in the flour and cold water until it forms a paste. Then stir into the hot chicken stock, stirring constantly until the mixture is smooth and boils.

Heat the milk over low heat, but do not let boil. When hot, stir the milk into the soup. Stir in the seasonings, and the sherry. simmer over low heat for 10 minutes and serve.

Serves 6 to 8.

TIP: *Wash the peelings from potatoes and carrots, and the tops from celery, and instead of throwing them away put them in a large soup pot, cover with water, add a little salt and cook over medium heat for an hour or so. Strain and use as a soup stock. Excellent used half and half with chicken stock for most soup recipes that call for chicken stock.*

Hopi Scalloped Red Peppers and Corn

4 cups fresh WHITE CORN, cut off the cob
2 fresh and firm RED CHILE peppers, finely chopped
1 can (10¾ oz.) condensed CREAM OF CELERY SOUP
½ cup EVAPORATED MILK
1 tsp. GARLIC SALT
½ tsp. ground WHITE PEPPER
½ tsp. DRY MUSTARD
1½ cups dry BREAD CRUMBS
½ cup melted BUTTER

Mix corn and chile together in a saucepan. Add the soup, milk, salt, pepper and mustard. Stir and cook over low heat until heated through.

In a mixing bowl, mix the bread crumbs and melted butter together. Line the bottom of a medium-sized baking dish with half of bread crumbs. Pour hot corn mixture over bread crumbs and cover with remaining crumbs. Bake in a 375 degree oven for 30 minutes.

Goes very well with roast pork.   Serves 6 to 8.

Corn Casserole

4 EGGS
½ cup all-purpose FLOUR
2 cans (10-oz. each) CREAMED CORN
1 cup HALF and HALF
½ cup chopped, cooked HAM
2 Tbsp. BUTTER
½ tsp. GARLIC SALT
¼ tsp. ground WHITE PEPPER
½ cup diced GREEN CHILE (fresh or canned)

Beat the eggs well, add rest of the ingredients, and put into a well-greased two-quart casserole dish. Put the dish in a pan of water in the oven and bake at 350 degrees for 45 minutes or until set.   Serves 6.

Pemmican

Plains Indians used this highly-concentrated food for energy, especially on long trips. They carried a small amount at a time in deerskin pouches, usually tied to their waists.

Here is a modern version of this practical food. It is a good addition to the supplies taken on a camping or hunting trip.

> 4 lbs. cured BEEF (or jerky)
> 1½ lbs. fresh PORK FAT
> 1 cup dried APRICOTS

Cut the fat into small pieces and cook in a skillet until melted. Grind beef until fine and mix with the fat until it is the consistency of sausage. Run the dried apricots through a grinder or food processor until finely chopped. Mix with meat mixture and shape into small balls.

Most of what Indians ate they had to either catch or kill. Deer were very plentiful in New Mexico and were a welcome addition to the diet.

Venison Steak con Chile

4 tsp. all-purpose FLOUR
2 tsp. RED CHILE POWDER
1 tsp. PAPRIKA
½ tsp. CELERY SALT
½ tsp. GARLIC SALT
¼ tsp. ground BLACK
  PEPPER

2½ to 3 lbs. VENISON
  STEAK, 1-inch thick
2 Tbsp. COOKING OIL
1 small yellow ONION,
  chopped
1 can (10-oz.) TOMATOES

Mix flour with chile powder, paprika, celery salt, garlic salt and pepper. Dredge steak in flour and seasonings. Heat oil in a heavy frying pan and saute the onion until barely soft. Add steak and brown very well on both sides. Add tomatoes and enough water to cover. Cover the pan and cook over low heat for 1½ hours or until done.   Serves 4.

Lamb Roast

"They dry a great quantity of mutton and use a great deal of common field corn. The corn is prepared for the winter by parboiling it in the shuck and drying it. They dry a great many peaches and melons from which the rinds and seeds have been removed."

—Pearl Cherry Miller on the New Mexican Indians
June 1, 1904

4 to 5 lbs. LAMB ROAST
1 tsp. ground BLACK PEPPER
8 to 10 cloves GARLIC

Preheat oven to 500 degrees. Rub meat with the pepper. Cut small pockets in the meat and insert garlic cloves. Put the roast in a baking pan and bake for 15 minutes at 500 degrees. Reduce heat to 350 degrees and cook for another two hours and 15 minutes or until the roast is done to taste.   Serves 6 to 8.

Comanche Frog Legs

½ cup CORNMEAL
½ tsp. SALT
¼ tsp. ground BLACK
   PEPPER
¼ tsp. GARLIC POWDER
1 EGG
8 med.-size FROG LEGS
½ cup COOKING OIL

Mix cornmeal, salt, pepper and garlic powder together. Beat the egg and stir into the cornmeal. Wash frog legs under cold running water and pat dry with paper toweling. Put the cooking oil in a large skillet and heat over medium-high flame. Dip the frog legs into cornmeal, coating well, and fry for 20 minutes until brown on all sides.   Serves 4.

Indian-Style Pinto Beans

Ah, beans! A New Mexican loves pinto beans! He may eat the kidney, navy and stringed varieties, but when it comes to a showdown in the kitchen, the pinto bean will always win.

Slow-simmered with just the right spices, a little bacon fat, and stirred lovingly by "Mamacita," the pinto bean has long been the foundation upon which many a New Mexican meal is built.

1 lb. dried PINTO BEANS
3 qts. WATER
½ lb. BACON, cut into pieces
1 med.-size yellow ONION, finely-chopped

1 tsp. GARLIC SALT
1 tsp. SALT
1 tsp. ground BLACK PEPPER
2 tsp. dried RED CHILE POWDER

Wash the beans thoroughly, removing any stones or bad beans. Soak overnight in cold water, changing the water at least once. Cook the bacon for a few minutes, add onion and cook until transparent. Put the beans into a large pot with the bacon and onion, cover with water and simmer, covered, for four hours or until beans start to soften. Add garlic salt, salt, pepper and chile powder, and cook for 30 minutes. Serve hot.

Serves 6 to 8.

TIP: *Refried beans are a wonderful accompaniment to many chile dishes and are easy to make. Scoop the beans, with a slotted kitchen spoon, from the juice they were cooked in. Heat a cast-iron skillet with a little bacon drippings, or lard, and add the beans and mash them with a potato masher. Stir them and cook over low heat until they are thick. Season with a little garlic salt, sprinkle cheese on the hot beans and serve.*

Tecolote Squash

Like so many dishes served over the years in New Mexico this one is a perfect marriage of Indian and Mexican influence.

2 to 3 med.-size yellow
  crook-neck SQUASH
  (about ¾-lb.)
2 Tbsp. BUTTER
1 small ONION, chopped
2 cloves GARLIC, minced
2 fresh TOMATOES,
  peeled and chopped
1 can (10 oz.) whole
  kernel CORN
½ tsp. SALT

2 Tbsp. chopped
  GREEN CHILE
  (fresh or canned)
¼ tsp. OREGANO
½ tsp. ground CUMIN
¼ tsp. ground BLACK
  PEPPER
1 cup LIGHT CREAM
¼ tsp. TABASCO® SAUCE
3 oz. CREAM CHEESE,
  cut into small cubes

In a heavy skillet, melt butter and saute the onion and garlic over medium heat for five minutes. Cut the squash into one-quarter-inch thick round slices and saute for another five minutes. Add the tomatoes, corn and spices, and cook over low heat for 20 minutes, or until squash is nice and tender, stirring two or three times to prevent sticking or burning.

Stir in light cream, Tabasco sauce and cream cheese. Cook over low heat until heated through. Serve hot.　　Serves 4.

Indian Fry Bread

New Mexico Indians prepare a delicious pastry they call "Fry Bread."

It is sold at many of the Pueblos and at art fairs, and ceremonial dances held throughout the year.

3 cups all-purpose FLOUR   ½ tsp. SALT
1⅓ cups warm WATER   LARD or COOKING OIL
1¼ tsp. BAKING POWDER   to fry in

Mix dry ingredients together, add warm water and knead until dough is soft but not sticky. Pat and stretch the dough until it is quite thin. Tear off a piece five or six inches square, poke a hole through the middle and drop into a pan of hot cooking oil. Brown on both sides and serve hot with butter or jam.

Makes 6 to 8 pieces.

Piñon Nut Muffins

Nuts and berries were an integral part of a New Mexican Indian's diet. Piñons, which grow in northern New Mexico, are hard to harvest and shell, but have a wonderful flavor.

1½ cups all-purpose FLOUR   ½ cup MILK
1 Tbsp. BAKING POWDER   1 cup PIÑON NUTS
¼ cup HONEY   pinch of SALT
½ cup SOUR CREAM   splash of BOURBON

Preheat oven to 425 degrees. Sift flour and baking powder together. Mix together the honey, sour cream, milk, nuts and seasonings. Combine with dry ingredients and fill each cup of a greased muffin tin halfway. Bake for 30 minutes at 375 degrees or until just golden brown.   Makes 10 to 12 muffins.

Indian Pudding

3 cups MILK
2/3 cup dark MOLASSES
2/3 cup yellow CORNMEAL
1/3 cup SUGAR

½ tsp. SALT
1 tsp. CINNAMON
½ tsp. NUTMEG
¼ cup BUTTER
1 cup MILK

Preheat oven to 300 degrees. Put three cups milk and the molasses into a saucepan and heat over low heat. Gradually stir the cornmeal, sugar, salt, cinnamon and nutmeg into milk mixture. Cut the butter into cubes and stir into mixture. Cook over low heat, stirring constantly until the mixture thickens (about 10 minutes).

Pour into a lightly-greased two-quart casserole or baking dish. Pour remaining cup of milk over the pudding. DO NOT STIR! Bake for three hours in a 300-degree oven. Serve hot with whipped cream.   Serves 4 to 6.

Squaw Cake

1 Tbsp. LARD
2 cups FLOUR

½ tsp. SALT
1½ tsp. BAKING POWDER

Mix all ingredients together with enough water to form a rather thin batter that runs slowly from a spoon. Grease a cast-iron skillet and heat it on top of the stove until it is very hot, then pour the batter into the skillet and return to the heat until the cake rises and is cooked on one side. Turn the cake over and brown well. This is very good with butter and jam.

Serves 4 to 6.

Indian Sugar Cookies

3 cups LARD
2 cups SUGAR
1 EGG
1/3 cup ROSÉ WINE

4 to 5 cups all-purpose
  FLOUR
½ cup SUGAR
¼ cup CINNAMON

Preheat oven to 350 degrees. Cream lard and sugar together. Beat the egg into them. Add wine and stir. Mix in four cups of the flour, adding more as needed until the dough rolls out easily. Roll dough out and cut into circles, about two inches in diameter, and put on a lightly-greased baking sheet. Mix the half-cup sugar with the cinnamon and sprinkle on top of the cookies.

Bake in a 350-degree oven for 10 minutes or until the cookies are lightly browned.

Makes approximately three dozen cookies.

TIP: *The children of New Mexico love pumpkin seeds—called pepitas in Spanish. They are easy to make. Just scoop the seeds from the pumpkin, remove as much of the white membrane as possible and spread in a single layer on an ungreased cookie sheet. Bake in a 300-degree oven for 15 to 20 minutes, stirring every five minutes, until they are a nice golden brown.*

CHAPTER TWO

The Influence of Old Mexico on the food of New Mexico

The Spaniards are Coming...The Spaniards Are Coming!

It would make a good movie! The hero is shipwrecked, captured by Indians, endures a trek of hundreds of miles in an often barren and hostile environment, and months of near starvation. All of this happened to Cabeza de Vaca, but he managed to become the first white man to ever see New Mexico when he entered the Land of Enchantment in 1535.

Five years later, resplendent in gold plated armor, Francisco Vasquez de Coronado came to New Mexico in search of the fabled "Seven Cities of Gold."

He headed a contingent of some three hundred soldiers, and a retinue of priests, Indian and Negro servants, Spanish noblemen, and hangers-on. He had borrowed a large sum of money, estimated to be over a million dollars in today's terms, from his wealthy wife Beatriz in order to finance this expedition.

The dream Coronado and his group were chasing seems to many historians to have been a figment of the imagination of a Franciscan monk, Friar Marcos de Niza. Fray Marcos had been sent north from Mexico City by the Viceroy Don Antonio de Mendoza officially to extend the sphere of influence of the Catholic faith.

Unofficially, everyone including the Viceroy was panting after riches in *Nueva Mexia* that would equal or surpass those found by Cortez in *Mexia*.

Mexia was the word that the Aztecs used to describe themselves and Cortez had named his newly-found land after them. When the Spanish extended their conquest north and hoped to find the same riches there, they optimistically named the territory Nueva Mexia or New Mexico.

Marcos was an experienced explorer and had been with the de Vaca expedition. The Viceroy assumed that a simple priest would cause less trouble with the Indians than obvious military men and be a lot less damaging to the King's purse.

Marcos had not penetrated into New Mexico very far when he turned tail and fled back to Mexico. His servant and scout had been killed by the Indians. The priest had feared for his own life and hastily beat it back to familiar territory.

It could well be that when he returned, this tale of bejeweled cities where the streets were "paved with gold" was his way of turning a failure into a success.

Coronado never did find the legendary golden cities, although he marched all the way through New Mexico, Colorado and on to eastern Kansas. The city that Marcos had originally seen from a distance and which he led Coronado to as the first of the mythical seven was but a simple Indian pueblo. The only treasures it had to offer the explorers were some meager food stuffs and water.

Coronado returned to Spain broke and in disgrace. However, he had paved the way for the influence of Spain and Mexico to be engraved on the new territory. The food in New Mexico reflects that heritage to this day.

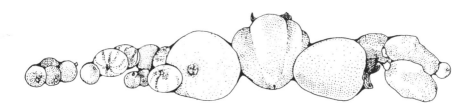

Some of the best soups I've ever tasted were in Mexico. Mexican cooks have a decided feel for making different and extremely tasty soups.

Cheese Soup

¼ cup BUTTER
½ cup finely-diced ONION
½ cup finely-diced CELERY
¼ cup all-purpose FLOUR
1½ Tbsp. CORNSTARCH
4 cups CHICKEN STOCK
4 cups MILK

⅛ tsp. BAKING SODA
1 cup VELVEETA®,
    cut in cubes
¼ tsp. ground
    BLACK PEPPER
¼ tsp. GARLIC SALT
2 Tbsp. finely-chopped
    PARSLEY

Melt butter in a pot large enough to hold all the ingredients. Saute onions and celery over low heat until soft. Then add the flour and cornstarch and stir until it bubbles. Gradually add chicken stock and milk and stir until smooth. Add soda, cheese, pepper and garlic salt. Cook over low heat until the cheese melts and blends into the mixture. Add the parsley, cook for five minutes more and then serve.   Serves 8.

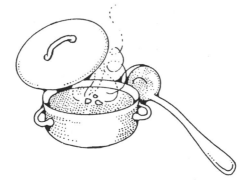

Sopa de Albondigas
(Meatball Soup)

1 lb. ground BEEF
1 tsp. GARLIC SALT
½ tsp. CELERY SALT
1 tsp. ground RED
  CHILE POWDER
1 cup dry fine
  BREAD CRUMBS
1 EGG

1 small YELLOW ONION,
  finely-chopped
½ cup PINE NUTS
  (optional)
2 cans (10½ oz. each)
  condensed BEEF
  CONSOMME
2 soup cans WATER
1 BAY LEAF

Mix together ground beef, garlic salt, celery salt, chile powder and bread crumbs. Beat the egg and stir into mixture. Add onion and pine nuts, mix well and shape into small balls. Bring the consomme, water and bay leaf to a boil in a large saucepan. Add the meat balls, a few at a time, so that boiling remains constant. After all the meat balls are in, reduce the heat, cover and simmer for 30 minutes. Remove bay leaf and serve.

Serves 4 to 6.

Green Pepper Consomme

3 large green BELL
  PEPPERS
3 large roasted, peeled,
  chopped GREEN CHILES
2 med.-size GREEN
  TOMATOES
1 med.-size WHITE ONION

½ tsp. SALT
¼ tsp. GROUND CLOVES
¼ tsp. ground WHITE
  PEPPER
2 cloves peeled GARLIC, run
  through a garlic press
2 qts. WATER
2 BEEF BOUILLON cubes

Cut away stems and take out fibers and seeds of bell peppers and dice. Remove stems of the tomatoes and dice. Mix all of the ingredients together in a large pan, bring to a boil, reduce the heat and let simmer for two hours. Then strain, discard the pulp, and serve the clear consomme hot. Serves 6.

Avocado-Mushroom Soup

2 Tbsp. BUTTER
1 Tbsp. LEMON JUICE
1 cup fresh, sliced
  MUSHROOMS
¼ tsp. ground WHITE
  PEPPER

¼ tsp. SALT
2 med.-size AVOCADOS
3 cups CHICKEN STOCK
1 tsp. CURRY POWDER
1 cup HALF and HALF

Melt butter in a small frying pan, stir in lemon juice and saute mushrooms for three or four minutes. Stir in salt and pepper. Peel avocados and remove pits. Cut up and mash in a blender. Add one cup of the chicken stock and blend. Transfer avocado mixture to a large saucepan and stir in remainder of stock. Add mushrooms. Stir in curry powder and half-and-half and heat through.   Serves 4.

TIP: *A little lime or lemon juice drizzled over avocado slices will help keep them from turning brown. Also, mix a little lime or lemon juice in mashed avocado dip or guacamole to keep it from turning a dark color.*

Cream of Potato Soup au Gratin

2 Tbsp. BUTTER
1 med.-size yellow ONION
4 large white POTATOES
½ cup chopped GREEN
   CHILE (fresh or canned)
2 cups CHICKEN STOCK
½ tsp. SALT
½ tsp. CELERY SALT

¼ tsp. ground WHITE
   PEPPER
1 cup MILK
1 cup LIGHT CREAM
6 Tbsp. grated CHEDDAR
   CHEESE
PARMESAN CHEESE
PAPRIKA

Melt butter in a saucepan. Peel and chop onion and saute in butter until soft. Peel and dice potatoes and stir into pan with the onion.

Then add chile, chicken stock, salt, celery salt and pepper and cook for 20 minutes, or until the potatoes are tender. Let cool. Then puree in a blender. Return to pan, add milk and cream and heat through.

When ready to serve, pour into individual flame-proof bowls and top with tablespoon of grated Cheddar cheese, dust with Parmesan cheese and sprinkle with paprika. Put the bowls under the broiler until cheese is bubbly and brown.

Serves 6.

Dry Soup

1 lb. CHORIZO
½ cup LARD (or cooking oil)
½ med.-size white or yellow ONION
2 cups uncooked long-grain WHITE RICE
½ cup TOMATO PUREE

4 cups BEEF BROTH
¼ tsp. ground black PEPPER
¼ tsp. GARLIC SALT
½ tsp. minced PARSLEY
2 EGGS, hard cooked
1 large, ripe AVOCADO

Remove outer casing from chorizo. Heat lard (or oil) in a frying pan and brown chorizo. Remove from pan, and mash. Brown onion in the pan, add rice and brown. Stir in the tomato puree, beef broth, pepper, garlic salt and parsley. Return chorizo to pan. Cook over medium heat for 25 to 30 minutes, or until rice is fluffy.

Turn into a serving dish. Slice the eggs. Peel, pit and slice the avocado. Arrange the egg slices and avocado slices on top of the rice.   Serves 4 to 6.

Menudo

Although usually classified as a soup, most New Mexicans can make an entire meal of menudo.

4 qts. WATER
2 BEEF KNUCKLES
2 Tbsp. dried PARSLEY
6 cloves GARLIC
2 lbs. TRIPE
1 Tbsp. BAKING SODA
2 med.-size white or yellow ONIONS, finely-chopped
1 tsp. MARJORAM
1 tsp. ground OREGANO
1 tsp. ground BLACK PEPPER

1 tsp. ground CUMIN
1 Tbsp. ground RED CHILE POWDER
½ cup chopped fresh CILANTRO
3 cups canned HOMINY
4 GREEN ONIONS, finely-chopped
6 LIME WEDGES

Wash beef knuckles thoroughly and put with water in a large pot. Add parsley. Peel and halve two of the garlic cloves and add. Cook for two hours over medium heat.

Wash tripe very well! Cut into pieces about one inch wide. Sprinkle soda over tripe in a large bowl and cover with cold water. Soak the tripe for 30 minutes. Drain the tripe and add to beef knuckles. Add onions. Peel and run the remaining garlic cloves through a garlic press and add to pot along with the marjoram, oregano, pepper, cumin and chile powder. Simmer for four hours on low heat.

Drain hominy and rinse under cold water. Add to tripe mixture and simmer for two more hours on low heat. Serve in large bowls, with green onions sprinkled on top and lime wedges on the side.   Serves 6.

Sinister Stew

2 med.-size yellow or white ONIONS
2 Tbsp. VEGETABLE OIL
2 lbs. LAMB STEW MEAT cut into chunks
4 cloves GARLIC
2 BAY LEAVES
¼ tsp. ground THYME
1 cup RED WINE
½ tsp. dried PARSLEY
½ tsp. ground BLACK PEPPER
¾ cup chopped GREEN CHILE (fresh or canned)
1 or 2 Tbsp. chopped JALAPEÑOS (to taste)

Peel and chop the onions, heat oil in a large pan and saute the onions for five minutes. Add rest of ingredients to the onions and cook, covered, over very low heat for four to five hours, or until the lamb is nice and tender. Remove bay leaves and garlic cloves and serve.

Served with rice and bread, this makes an excellent, albeit hot, dish.   Serves 6 to 8.

Stuffed Rolls

6 good-size dinner ROLLS
1 lb. GROUND BEEF
¼ cup chopped yellow ONION
½ tsp. GARLIC POWDER
½ tsp. ONION SALT
1 POTATO, finely-shredded
4 med. hot GREEN CHILES
½ cup processed AMERICAN CHEESE, cut into small pieces
2 Tbsp. COOKING OIL

Cut tops off rolls and remove the dough from the center, leaving a shell. (Save the dough from the rolls to use in another dish as bread crumbs.)

In a frying pan saute together the beef, onions, garlic powder, onion salt, shredded potato and chile in the oil until done. Stir in cheese and mix until cheese melts. Stuff rolls with the mixture, put the tops back on and keep in a warm oven until ready to serve.   Serves 6.

Avocado and Papaya Salad

½ head of BOSTON
  LETTUCE, washed
  and dried
½ bunch WATERCRESS,
  washed and dried
2 ripe AVOCADOS
1 Tbsp. fresh LEMON JUICE

1 ripe PAPAYA, peeled,
  seeded and sliced
¼ cup finely-chopped
  PECANS
½ cup virgin OLIVE OIL
¼ cup TARRAGON
  VINEGAR

Break lettuce and watercress by hand into bite size pieces and put into a glass salad bowl. Peel avocados, remove the pit and slice. Rub slices with lemon juice and add to the bowl. Add papaya slices and pecans. Mix together olive oil and vinegar very well and pour over the salad, tossing lightly.   Serves 4.

Ensalada Mexicana
(Mexican Salad)

3 large GREEN BELL
  PEPPERS,
  coarsely-chopped
4 med.-size ripe TOMATOES,
  cut into bite-size pieces
1 med.-size white or yellow
  ONION

LETTUCE LEAVES
4 slices BACON, cut into
  bite-size pieces
1 tsp. RED CHILE POWDER
½ cup RED WINE VINEGAR

Lightly toss peppers, tomatoes and onion together and put on a platter or into a shallow salad bowl lined with the lettuce leaves.

Cook the bacon in a frying pan until it starts to crisp up. Turn off heat. Add chile powder and vinegar. Stir well. Pour over the vegetables and serve.   Serves 4 to 6.

Mexican Omelet

¼ cup diced yellow ONION
3 large fresh MUSHROOMS
1 tsp. BUTTER
3 EGGS
¼ tsp. PEPPER
dash SALT
¼ tsp. MILK

HOT PEPPER SAUCE
¼ cup jalapeño-flavored
    processed AMERICAN
    CHEESE, cubed
1 tsp. RED SALSA (very hot)
2 strips crisp BACON,
    crumbled

Saute onions and mushrooms together in the butter. Take out of the pan and reserve.

Beat eggs, add pepper, salt, milk and hot pepper sauce. Put into the same pan over medium heat. Sprinkle the cheese over egg mixture. Add onions and mushrooms and spread salsa over the top. Sprinkle the bacon on top and cook until moist and set but not hard.

Serve as is or with tomato salsa and a warm flour tortilla.

Serves 1.

Boss Salsa

4 large fresh ripe red
    TOMATOES, coarsely-
    chopped
2 TOMATILLOS,
    coarsely-chopped
1 large WHITE ONION,
    finely-chopped
4 oz. chopped GREEN CHILE
1 clove peeled GARLIC, run
    through a garlic press

3 Tbsp. OLIVE OIL
3 Tbsp. RED WINE VINEGAR
2 tsp. minced fresh
    CILANTRO
½ tsp. GARLIC SALT
½ tsp. ground BLACK
    PEPPER
¼ tsp. ground OREGANO

Mix all ingredients together and chill. Serve with tortilla chips or as a side dish with meat.

Makes approximately two cups.

Marinated Onions

3 large RED ONIONS
½ cup SALAD OIL
2 Tbsp. LEMON JUICE
2 Tbsp. chopped
  GREEN CHILE
½ tsp. SALT

½ tsp. GARLIC SALT
½ tsp. PAPRIKA
½ tsp. SUGAR
¼ cup BLUE CHEESE,
  crumbled

Peel and slice the onions. Combine remaining ingredients (except the cheese). Stir well and pour over onions. Then stir in the cheese. Toss carefully with a fork and refrigerate for at least two days in a covered dish.   Serves 4 to 6.

Terrific Tacos

Tacos are the Mexican equivalent of a sandwich. A cornmeal tortilla is filled with meat, beans and/or cheese. The great debate in our household is always whether to make the tacos with ground meat or shredded beef. Either way is great. Here is the ground meat recipe.

2 Tbsp. BACON DRIPPINGS
1 lb. lean GROUND BEEF
½ med.-size yellow ONION,
  coarsely-chopped
½ tsp. GARLIC SALT
½ tsp. ground CUMIN
½ tsp. SALT
½ tsp. ground BLACK
  PEPPER

COOKING OIL
12 CORN TORTILLAS
½ lb. grated LONGHORN
  (or cheddar) CHEESE
1 cup shredded LETTUCE
½ cup finely-chopped
  fresh TOMATO

Heat the bacon drippings in a frying pan. Cook the onions for a couple of minutes, add the beef and brown with the garlic salt, cumin, salt and pepper.

Heat the cooking oil in another frying pan, and quickly fry the tortillas until limp. Drain on paper towels, put a spoonful of the meat mixture in each, fold and top with the lettuce, tomatoes and cheese. Serve with your favorite picante sauce.   Serves 4.

Mexican Flag Enchilada Plate

Dip three corn tortillas into hot oil for just a moment. Then dip one in green chile sauce, one in red chile sauce and leave the other plain.

Fill each tortilla with Beef Enchilada Filling. Roll the tortillas with the stuffing inside and place side by side on a plate. Sauce one with the green chile sauce, one with the red chile sauce, and put sour cream on the third. Top this last one with a few pieces of chopped black olive. Serve with rice and beans and you have the perfect, colorful "sampler" for those new to the Southwest.

Serves 1.

Beef Enchilada Filling

¼ large ONION, finely-chopped
1 Tbsp. BACON DRIPPINGS
1 lb. GROUND BEEF
½ tsp. ground CUMIN
½ tsp. GARLIC SALT
½ tsp. SALT
½ tsp. ground BLACK PEPPER
¼ cup chopped GREEN CHILE (fresh or canned)
1 tsp. ground RED CHILE POWDER
1 cup grated CHEDDAR CHEESE

Saute the chopped onion in the bacon drippings for a couple of minutes, then stir in the ground beef. Add the rest of the ingredients and cook until the meat is brown and cooked through. Fill the tortillas for the Mexican Flag Enchilada Plate with the meat mixture and a little grated cheese.

For 4 Mexican Flag Enchilada Plates.

Shrimp al Ajillo

When I lived in Spain I learned to cook this favorite Spanish dish. When I moved to New Mexico and was experimenting with chile, I found that green chile makes this dish really sing. Be sure and serve it with rice and lots of French bread to sop up the garlic oil.

¼ cup virgin OLIVE OIL
6 cloves GARLIC, peeled
   and cut horizontally
   into thick slices

36 large SHRIMP,
   peeled and deveined
½ cup chopped GREEN
   CHILE (fresh or canned)
LIME WEDGES

Heat the olive oil in a large heavy frying pan or wok until it is very, very hot. Add the garlic, reduce the heat and cook the garlic until it starts to brown and soften.

Add the shrimp and chile, and cook for about seven minutes or until they turn pink. Do not cook too long or they will be tough. Serve hot and squeeze lime wedges over the shrimp for a wonderful taste.   Serves 6.

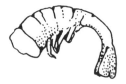

TIP: *Vegetable oil has a less distinct flavor and a higher smoking point than olive oil. Olive oil is usually more expensive so a combination of the two will enhance the flavor of a dish and help keep the budget in line.*

Scallops in Mushroom/Chile Sauce

16 small bay SCALLOPS
2 BAY LEAVES
¼ tsp. ground WHITE
   PEPPER
½ cup MILK
1 small white ONION
3 Tbsp. BUTTER
2 Tbsp. all-purpose FLOUR

½ cup heavy CREAM
1 clove minced GARLIC
½ Tbsp. TEQUILA
8 small MUSHROOMS
½ cup chopped GREEN
   CHILE (fresh or canned)
BREADCRUMBS
½ tsp. PAPRIKA

Put the scallops, bay leaf, white pepper and milk in a sauce pan and simmer over very low heat for five minutes. Remove scallops and strain the milk and save. Cut each scallop into two pieces.

Chop onion finely, melt butter in a large heavy pan and saute the onion, then stir in the flour. Gradually add the warm milk and then the cream. Stir in garlic and tequila. Cook for five minutes over medium heat.

Clean and slice the mushrooms and add to the mixture. Stir in chile, and then add reserved scallops. Butter four ramekins and divide mixture into them. Top with breadcrumbs, dot with butter, sprinkle with paprika and place under broiler until nicely browned.   Serves 4.

Pork Medallions
and Scalloped Potatoes

4 large PORK CHOPS
2 Tbsp. COOKING OIL
4 cups peeled, thinly-sliced
POTATOES
1 can CREAM of CELERY
SOUP
1 cup MILK

2 Tbsp. chopped GREEN
CHILE (fresh or canned)
1 tsp. ground BLACK
PEPPER
1 tsp. SALT
2 tsp. dried DILL WEED
2 tsp. DRIED PARSLEY
1 tsp. PAPRIKA

Cut meat away from bone on each chop to make the pork medallions. Heat oil in frying pan, and brown pork medallions on each side. Transfer to bottom of lightly-buttered casserole dish and top with sliced potatoes. Mix soup with milk and then stir in chile, pepper, salt, dill weed and parsley. Pour this mixture over potatoes. Sprinkle top with paprika, and bake in a 350-degree oven for 90 minutes or until done.   Serves 4.

Spanish Rice

2 Tbsp. COOKING OIL
1 cup white long-grain RICE
2 cloves GARLIC (peeled)
1 small yellow ONION,
finely-chopped
2 cups crushed TOMATOES
1 cup WATER

1 tsp. coarse-ground
BLACK PEPPER
½ tsp. SALT
½ tsp. CELERY SALT
pinch OREGANO
pinch BASIL

Heat oil in large skillet or dutch oven, and fry rice in oil until brown. Run garlic through a garlic press and stir into the rice. Add onion. Stir in tomatoes and water. Add remaining ingredients. Cover and simmer over low heat for 30 minutes or until done.   Serves 4 to 6.

Mexican Bread Pudding

4 cups WATER
1 lb. light BROWN SUGAR
½ tsp. ground CINNAMON
½ tsp. ground CLOVES

8 slices white bread
  TOAST
1 cup seedless RAISINS
½ lb. Monterey Jack
  CHEESE, cubed

Mix water, brown sugar, cinnamon and cloves together in a saucepan, and bring to a boil. Boil until it forms a syrup. Generously butter a casserole or baking dish, and layer the toast, raisins and cheese. Pour water/sugar mixture over the top, and bake in a 350-degree oven for 30 minutes.

Serves 4 to 6.

Kahlua Souffle

2 half-cups MILK
1 Tbsp. unflavored GELATIN
4 EGG YOLKS
2 portions (1/3 cup each)
  SUGAR

pinch of SALT
½ tsp. CINNAMON
3 Tbsp. KAHLUA®
4 EGG WHITES
pinch CREAM of TARTAR

Put half cup milk in top of a double boiler, stir in gelatin until melted. Beat egg yolks, then add another half cup of milk and beat. Add to gelatin mixture. Cook in top of a double boiler over boiling water for about 10 minutes or until mixture starts to thicken. Remove from heat and stir in one-third cup of sugar, salt, cinnamon and Kahlua. Let cool.

Beat egg whites, adding cream of tartar and one-third cup sugar halfway through beating and beat until they form stiff peaks. Fold egg whites into gelatin mixture, pour into a four-cup souffle dish and chill overnight.

Serves 4 to 6.

Champaña Pera

1 oz. PEAR NECTAR
1 tsp. SUGAR

dash of ANGOSTURA®
BITTERS
4 oz. CHAMPAGNE

Moisten rim of a champagne glass with a little of the pear nectar. Put sugar on a small plate and roll rim of glass in sugar.

Pour rest of pear nectar in bottom of the glass, stir in bitters, add champagne and drink. Makes 1 drink.

TIP: *Having a party and don't know what to serve? Pop up a large supply of popcorn, sprinkle with parmesan cheese and Tabasco® Sauce, toss lightly and serve.*

CHAPTER THREE

Chile is a Way of Life

New Mexico is one of the leading growers of chile and New Mexicans are extremely proud of their large consumption of it.

The myriad qualities of chile practically defy efforts of categorizing. The plants themselves can freely cross-pollinate, producing hot and mild peppers on the same plant. They come in various shapes including tapered, round and conical. The colors of chile vary from green to red, yellow, white, orange, brown and black and can even change while on the vine.

Chiles can be used raw, canned, pickled or powdered. They are sweet, mild or fire-breathing hot to the taste. A high content of vitamin C, plus large quantities of vitamin A and essential minerals are found in chile. In addition to being used for food, chile is also often used for decorative purposes. A chile *ristra*, or string of chiles, is a common sight in New Mexico.

The following descriptions include the most popular chiles grown in New Mexico, as well as some less common varieties:

BELL PEPPER: Is the most common member of the CAPSICUM (chile) group. It is bell-shaped, green or yellow maturing to red on the vine, and is mild or sweet to the taste.

PIMIENTO: This red, European, heart-shaped CAPSICUM is thick-fleshed and sweeter than red bell pepper. Usually canned, or a source of "paprika," it is also delicious when used fresh in many dishes.

PAPRIKA: A green, conical, three to five-inch long chile which turns red on the vine, and is usually ground into powder. These plants vary widely, as do the New Mexican varieties, and are a major ingredient in Hungarian cooking. Any variety of finely-ground sweet peppers is often referred to as "paprika."

CALIFORNIA or ANAHEIM: When fresh, this chile is a bright, shiny green which matures to red. It tapers from five to eight inches long and varies in taste from sweet to mild and mildly hot.

CAYENNE: Green or red and very hot! This chile is about three inches long, thin and tapered. Often many varieties of hot peppers, when ground, are called "cayenne."

PASILLA: A long, thin, tapered seven to 12-inch long, dark green chile, which ripens to dark brown and brownish-black when dried.

YELLOW CHILES: These chiles, which can be used either fresh or pickled, include Hungarian or Armenian wax (shaped like the regular tapered chile), banana pepper, the small floral gem types which are very hot, *caribe, cascabel*, and yellow wax.

ANCHO or POBLANO: This chile resembles the bell pepper but is more waxy, darker green and tapered. The flavor becomes sweeter as it ripens on the vine. Dried anchos are flat, wrinkled, brownish red to near black, and good for powder and sauces.

FRESNO: This conical-shaped chile is about two inches long, bright green changing to orange and then red on the vine, mildly hot to painful in taste, and is usually pickled.

JALAPENO: This oval-shaped chile is dark green about two to 2½ inches long, and very HOT! When Jalapeno peppers are sun-ripened, dried and smoked, they are called *chipotle*. Very popular now, and often used in place of "green chile," because they are usually cheaper.

BARKER: A New Mexican chile five to six inches long, tapered, thin-fleshed and very HOT!

SERRANO: Small, only one to 1½ inches long and cylindrical, this VERY HOT chile is a rich waxy green which changes to orange and then red on the vine. They are usually canned or pickled.

NEW MEXICO 6/4: This mildly-hot chile is thick-fleshed and tapers from six to eight inches.

RIO GRANDE 21: A favorite New Mexico chile. It is large, thick, tapered and mildly hot.

SANDIA A: A very hot, rough-surfaced, thick-tapered, six to seven-inch long chile.

NEW-MEX BIG JIM: Five of these fresh green chiles can weigh a pound! Tapered, seven to eight inches long, thick, and mildly hot. This chile is a favorite with a lot of New Mexican cooks when making chile rellenos.

NOTE: When using canned green chiles in recipes, their color will be moss-green and they will have a softer texture than fresh.

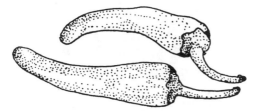

TIP: *When working with fresh green chile it is advisable to wear rubber or latex gloves. Otherwise the chiles can burn the skin. Certainly DO NOT rub your eyes with your hands when working with the chile.*

Chile con Queso

Nothing can kick off a party in New Mexico like homemade Chile Con Queso served with crisp tortilla chips.

1 lb. VELVEETA, chopped
    into cubes
½ can EVAPORATED MILK
4 oz. chopped GREEN
    CHILE (fresh or canned)

1 tsp. GARLIC SALT
½ tsp. CAYENNE PEPPER
¼ tsp. TABASCO SAUCE

Combine the ingredients in a saucepan and cook over very low heat, stirring occasionally, until the cheese is melted and warm through. Serve with tortilla chips.

The cheese can also be melted in a microwave.

Serves 10 to 12.

Chile Cheese Pinwheels

Great served as an appetizer at cocktail parties.

1 cup all-purpose FLOUR
2 cups sharp CHEDDAR
    CHEESE, coarsely-grated

¼ lb. BUTTER
2 cups chopped GREEN
    CHILE (fresh or canned)
1 Tbsp. BRANDY

Mix the flour and cheese together. Melt the butter and mix with the flour and cheese mixture. Knead until thoroughly blended. Then roll out in a rectangular shape, about ⅛-inch thick. Spread chile on top of dough. Sprinkle brandy on top of chile. Then roll the dough up like a jelly roll. Slice into rounds and bake in a 350-degree oven for 10 minutes or until lightly brown.   Makes approximately three dozen pinwheels.

Spinach & Green Chile Balls

You won't have to coax anybody to eat their spinach when you prepare it this way.

2 cups cooked chopped
  SPINACH
½ cup grated PARMESAN
  CHEESE
½ lb. RICOTTA CHEESE
2 EGGS
4 oz. chopped GREEN
  CHILE (fresh or canned)

½ tsp. ground BLACK
  PEPPER
½ tsp. GARLIC POWDER
¼ tsp. SALT
¼ tsp. ground NUTMEG
2 cups plain
  TOMATO SAUCE
3 Tbsp. grated ROMANO
  CHEESE

Drain the spinach very well. Combine all ingredients together EXCEPT tomato sauce and Romano cheese. Mix well and shape in meatball-size balls.

4 qts. WATER
1 Tbsp. SALT

Bring water to a boil, add salt and drop the balls into the water, six at a time. Cook for five minutes, counting the time from the moment the ball rises to the surface of the water. Lift the cooked balls out of water with a slotted spoon and put them on a warmed serving dish or platter.

In the meantime, heat tomato sauce. When all balls are cooked, cover with tomato sauce, sprinkle with Romano cheese and serve.   Serves 4 to 6.

TIP: *The "heat" in chile tends to increase when frozen—so adjust the amount used in recipes accordingly.*

Tomato & Green Chile Souffle

2 cups whole cooked,
  peeled TOMATOES
3 Tbsp. PEANUT OIL
3 Tbsp. all-purpose FLOUR
½ tsp. dried BASIL
½ tsp. DILL WEED

¼ tsp. ground WHITE
  PEPPER
¼ tsp. SALT (optional)
3 Tbsp. chopped GREEN
  CHILE
1 tsp. BAKING POWDER
5 egg YOLKS
5 egg WHITES

Run tomatoes through a blender or food processor and puree. Then blend with all other ingredients except egg whites. Beat egg whites until stiff. (Use a pinch of cream of tartar if they won't stiffen due to humidity.) Fold egg whites into the mixture and gently spoon into a lightly-buttered souffle dish. Bake in a 375-degree oven for 30 minutes. Serve immediately!

Serves 4 to 6.

Linguini with Green Chile Sauce

1 pkg. (12 oz.) LINGUINI
4 Tbsp. BUTTER
4 Tbsp. OLIVE OIL
4 cloves GARLIC, peeled
  and run through a
  garlic press

1/2 cup chopped GREEN
  CHILE

Cook linguini according to package directions. While it is cooking, melt butter in a saucepan, add olive oil, garlic and green chile and heat through. Drain linguini, put on a serving platter and pour sauce over it. Toss lightly and serve.

Serves 4 to 6

Salmon Loaf with Cucumber Chile Sauce

1 can (12½ oz.) SALMON, packed in water
½ cup MAYONNAISE
1 can (10¾ oz.) CREAM of CELERY SOUP
2 EGGS, beaten
1 cup CRACKER CRUMBS
¾ cup finely-chopped yellow ONION
¼ cup RED PEPPER FLAKES
1 Tbsp. LEMON JUICE
2 tsp. BAKING POWDER
2 tsp. PAPRIKA
1 tsp. CRAB CAKE SPICE (optional)

Drain and flake the salmon and put in a medium-size mixing bowl. Add rest of ingredients and pour into a lightly-greased loaf pan. Bake in 350-degree oven for one hour or until done. Serve hot with the following sauce.   Serves 4 to 6.

Cucumber Chile Sauce

1 med.-size CUCUMBER
½ cup SOUR CREAM
¼ cup MAYONNAISE
2 Tbsp. chopped GREEN CHILE
1 tsp. LEMON JUICE

Peel and finely-chop the cucumber. Mix with rest of ingredients and serve over salmon loaf.

Green Chile Chicken

1 med.-size yellow ONION
1 clove GARLIC, peeled
2 Tbsp. BACON DRIPPINGS
   (or cooking oil)
1 (3 to 3½ lb.) CHICKEN,
   cut into serving pieces

½ cup WATER
¼ cup TEQUILA
½ tsp. SALT
1 cup GREEN CHILE SAUCE
   (see recipe)

Peel and chop the onion coarsely, and dice the garlic. Saute in bacon drippings until onion is tender. Then put chicken into pan with water, tequila and salt. Simmer for 30 minutes, then add green chile sauce and simmer another hour or until done. Great served with rice.   Serves 4.

Ham and Scalloped Potatoes with Green Chile

3 cups cooked HAM,
   cut into bite-size cubes
3 GREEN ONIONS, chopped
½ cup diced GREEN CHILE
6 med.-size POTATOES,
   peeled, and thinly-sliced
3 Tbsp. BUTTER
3 Tbsp. all-purpose FLOUR

1 tsp. dried MUSTARD
2 cups MILK
1 tsp. SALT
1 tsp. ground BLACK
   PEPPER
¼ cup unseasoned
   BREAD CRUMBS
2 tsp. PAPRIKA

Mix together ham, onions and chile. Put a layer of sliced potatoes in a well-buttered baking dish and sprinkle some of the ham-and-chile mixture over them. Repeat until sliced potatoes and ham and chile mixture are all used.

Melt butter in a frying pan, whisk in flour and then slowly pour in milk, whisking constantly until mixture is smooth and starts to thicken. Whisk in mustard, salt and pepper, and then pour over potato mixture. Top with bread crumbs, sprinkle paprika on top, cover and bake in a 375-degree oven for one hour. Uncover and bake for 30 more minutes or until potatoes are done.   Serves 4.

Baked Halibut with Green Chile

4 HALIBUT filets
2 Tbsp. melted BUTTER
½ tsp. PAPRIKA
½ cup chopped TOMATOES
½ cup chopped
   GREEN ONIONS
¼ tsp. ground
   WHITE PEPPER
¼ cup dry WHITE WINE
¼ cup chopped GREEN
   CHILE
½ cup CREAM

Rinse the halibut under cold water, pat dry with a paper towel and lay filets in a baking pan. Pour melted butter over them and sprinkle paprika on top. Combine rest of ingredients and pour around filets, not over them. Bake in a 375-degree oven for 10 minutes.

Baste with the liquid and bake for another 10 to 20 minutes or until done, depending on the thickness of filets, basting occasionally.   Serves 4.

Chorizo

1 lb. lean GROUND BEEF
1 lb. bulk "regular"
   PORK SAUSAGE
3 cloves GARLIC,
   finely-minced
1 small white ONION,
   finely-minced
3 Tbsp. RED CHILE
   POWDER
3 Tbsp. DISTILLED
   WHITE VINEGAR
1 tsp. ground OREGANO
½ tsp. SALT
½ tsp. ground BLACK
   PEPPER

Combine all ingredients and chill in refrigerator at least six hours. To serve, form into links, or patties and brown well in a heavy frying pan.   Serves 8 to 10.

Onion Pie

The recipe made by the frugal French housewives of Mora, New Mexico is a very simple variation of a quiche.

4 cups thinly-sliced ONIONS
3 Tbsp. BUTTER
2 EGGS
½ tsp. SALT
⅛ tsp. ground WHITE
  PEPPER
pinch of NUTMEG

1 deep dish PASTRY SHELL,
  baked for 10 min. in
  400-degree oven
½ cup SOUR CREAM
2 Tbsp. SWEET CREAM
½ cup chopped
  GREEN CHILE

Preheat oven to 325 degrees. Saute onions in butter over low heat until they are soft and translucent. Do not brown. Lightly beat eggs, fold in onions and spices. Pour mixture into baked pastry shell. Mix sweet cream into the sour cream, add green chile and spoon on top of onions. Bake for 30 minutes at 325 degrees or until the top is set and a golden brown.   Serves 4.

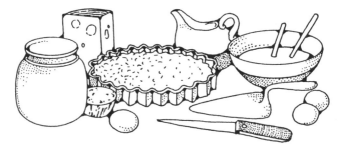

TIP: *Beer goes well with chile dishes. Try putting two or three ice cubes in the glass before pouring in the beer and serving it with a slice of lime.*

Chile Verde
(Green Chile)

2 lbs. BEEF (or VENISON)
2 lbs. PORK
¼ cup BACON DRIPPINGS
   (or COOKING OIL)
1 cup chopped ONION
2 cloves GARLIC
2 Tbsp. all-purpose FLOUR
1 to 2 cups chopped GREEN
   CHILE (depending on
   "heat" of chile)

1 tsp. ground BLACK
   PEPPER
½ tsp. OREGANO
½ tsp. dried PARSLEY
½ tsp. SALT
¼ tsp. CELERY SALT
1 can (10¾ oz.) BEEF
   BOUILLON
2 qts. WATER

Cut all meats into bite-sized pieces and brown in drippings or oil. Add onion and garlic, and cook until the onion is limp but not brown. Add flour and stir until it is blended in. Add rest of ingredients and cook until meat is tender, about two hours over a low-to-medium heat.   Serves 8 to 10.

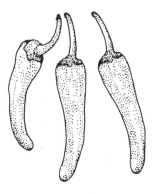

TIP: *If the chile you are eating is too HOT and burns your mouth—water alone won't put out the fire. So eat a piece of unbuttered bread.*

Carne Adobada

Carne Adobada, or pork chops marinated in red chile sauce, is a very popular dish in the northern part of New Mexico.

2 cups RED CHILE SAUCE
1 tsp. SALT
3 cloves GARLIC, run
through garlic press

1 tsp. OREGANO
12 PORK CHOPS
2 Tbsp. COOKING OIL

Stir seasonings into red chile and pour over pork chops. Put into refrigerator for at least twenty-four hours. Take pork chops out of marinade and reserve marinade. Fry chops in oil until brown on both sides. Pour marinade back over chops, cover, and cook over low heat for 30 minutes or until tender.

Serves 6.

Red Chile Sauce

This red chile sauce can be used for Carne Adobada or in making your red enchiladas.

24 to 30 dried RED CHILE PODS
4 to 5 cups WATER
1 tsp. SALT

Wash chile and remove stems and seeds. Combine chile and water in a saucepan and bring to a boil. Lower heat and cook for 15 minutes. Let cool and blend (in a blender) a small amount at a time. Then strain through a sieve and add salt. Store in refrigerator for immediate use, freeze remainder.

Makes 2 cups.

Corn and Bean Soup

2 BOUILLON CUBES
1 cup WATER
2 cups cooked PINTO
   BEANS in their own juice
1 can (10 oz.) creamed-
   style CORN
1 tsp. WORCESTERSHIRE
   SAUCE

¼ tsp. GARLIC SALT
½ tsp. ground BLACK
   PEPPER
1 Tbsp. RED CHILE
   POWDER

Dissolve bouillon cubes in water in a saucepan. Add rest of ingredients and simmer for 15 to 20 minutes or until flavors are blended through. Serves 6.

Chicken with Rice & Chile Stuffing

1 cup uncooked RICE
2 cups CHICKEN BROTH
1 small ONION
¼ lb. fresh MUSHROOMS
1½ Tbsp. melted BUTTER
1 cup diced CELERY
½ cup chopped GREEN CHILE
1 tsp. grated ORANGE RIND
1 Tbsp. PARSLEY
½ tsp. GINGER
¼ tsp. ground BLACK PEPPER
1 Tbsp. SOY SAUCE
1 tsp. GARLIC SALT
1 tsp. dried RED CHILE FLAKES
3½ to 4 lb. roasting CHICKEN

Cook rice according to package directions, substituting chicken broth for the required amount of water. Saute onion and mushrooms in butter for five minutes. Add celery and cook for another five minutes over low heat.

Stir cooked vegetables, green chile and seasonings into rice and stuff chicken. Roast for 1½ hours in a 325-degree oven or until chicken tests done, basting several times with the basting sauce.   Serves 4 to 6.

Basting Sauce

2 Tbsp. HONEY
2 Tbsp. SOY SAUCE
1 tsp. WINE VINEGAR
¼ cup WHITE WINE
¼ tsp. GARLIC SALT
½ tsp. RED CHILE POWDER

Mix all ingredients together to use in basting chicken.

Rice Salad

1 cup uncooked RICE
6 Tbsp. OLIVE OIL
3 Tbsp. WINE VINEGAR
1 tsp. LIME JUICE
1 tsp. SALT
1 tsp. ground BLACK
  PEPPER
½ tsp. TARRAGON
¼ cup sliced GREEN
  OLIVES stuffed with
  pimentos

¼ cup chopped GREEN
  CHILE (fresh or canned)
1 tsp. chopped,
  dried PARSLEY
½ cup CUCUMBER, cut into
  bite-sized pieces
¼ cup chopped
  GREEN ONIONS
1 Tbsp. chopped CHIVES
FRENCH DRESSING
  (see recipe)
SALAD GREENS
2 hard-cooked EGGS

Cook rice according to package directions. Mix while still hot with olive oil, vinegar, lime juice, salt, pepper and tarragon. Let stand until cool, then mix with green olives, green chile, parsley, cucumber, green onions and chives. Mix with French dressing to desired taste.

Make a bed of fresh salad greens, spoon the rice salad in the center and garnish with the hard-cooked eggs.   Serves 4.

French Dressing

1 tsp. ground BLACK
  PEPPER
1 tsp. SALT
1 tsp. PAPRIKA
½ tsp. DRY MUSTARD

dash CAYENNE PEPPER
¼ cup WHITE WINE
  VINEGAR
1 cup virgin OLIVE OIL
  (or vegetable oil)

Combine pepper, salt, paprika, mustard and cayenne with vinegar in a jar with a lid. Add oil, seal the jar and shake well. Serve at room temperature. Can be stored in refrigerator.

                    Approx. 1¼ cups.

Green Enchiladas

2½ to 3 lb. CHICKEN
2 Tbsp. COARSE (kosher) SALT
1 cup MILK
COOKING OIL
1 doz. CORN TORTILLAS
1 can (10¾ oz.) CREAM of CELERY SOUP
8 oz. chopped GREEN CHILE (fresh or canned)
1 large yellow ONION, chopped
½ tsp. GARLIC SALT
¼ tsp. ground BLACK PEPPER
½ tsp. CUMIN
1 lb. LONGHORN CHEESE, grated

Wash the chicken, place in a large mixing bowl with the coarse salt, cover with cold water and let stand for one hour. Drain chicken, put into large pot, cover with water, bring to a boil, reduce the heat and simmer for one hour or until chicken is very tender. Let cool enough to handle, remove skin and bones, and dice chicken. Mix soup with milk. Heat just enough cooking oil in a skillet to lightly coat each tortilla. Turn each tortilla in the hot oil just until soft and set aside.

In a greased baking dish, layer tortillas four at a time with one-fourth of each of the remaining ingredients, topping off with cheese each time. Bake in 350-degree oven for 30 minutes or until hot and bubbly.   Serves 4 to 6.

TIP: *If you are in a hurry to peel fresh green chile and you don't have time to roast it—drop it in boiling water for a minute or so until the skin starts to separate from the meat of the chile. Remove the chile from the water and peel.*

Green Chile Cheese Cornbread

1 cup YELLOW CORN MEAL
1 cup sifted all-purpose
  FLOUR
2 tsp. BAKING POWDER
¼ tsp. SALT
1 can (12 oz.) EVAPORATED
  MILK
¼ cup VEGETABLE OIL

1 EGG
1 can (4 oz.) chopped
  GREEN CHILE
1 can (17 oz.) whole kernel
  CORN, drained
1½ cups grated CHEDDAR
  CHEESE
2 tbsp. VEGETABLE OIL

Sift together corn meal, flour, baking powder and salt. Stir in milk, oil and egg. Beat well. Add chile, corn and cheese. Pour two tablespoons oil into a cast-iron skillet (or baking pan) and heat. Pour the batter into it, and bake in a 375-degree oven for 30 minutes, or until done.   Serves 8.

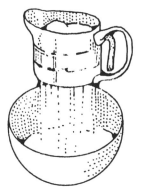

TIP: *When you open canned green chile and do not use it all at once—transfer it to either a tightly covered glass or plastic container. It will keep about a week in the refrigerator and approximately three months in the freezer.*

CHAPTER FOUR

The Mesilla Valley Legend

Amid a lot of fanfare, speech-making and a flag raising ceremony, a treaty was signed on November 16, 1854, determining that the Gadsden Purchase, a narrow strip of land that had been hotly disputed between the sovereign powers Mexico and the United States, was now officially part of the United States.

The proceedings, held in the town plaza of La Mesilla, signaled the rapid growth of the small settlement. Mesilla became an important stopover for the Butterfield Overland Mail and Stage Line and rapidly became the focus of the social, business and legal activities in the southern part of New Mexico.

The *Mesilla Times* was the first newspaper printed in the entire area. In the first issue, October 18, 1860, the following appeared describing Mesilla's rapid development.

"In this valley, which was believed by the Mexican people to be the Garden of Eden, is located the town of Mesilla. Up to about three years ago her increase in size and population was comparatively slow and steady. Since that time, however, her progress has been very rapid indeed. By far the largest portion of the town has sprung into existence during these last three years—where before could be seen only a few scattered jacales, with now and then a solitary adobe, now is found a population of some 2,500 people with many large stores, several beautiful dwellings, and a due number of public buildings."

Today, fancy boutiques, art galleries, gourmet food stores, restaurants and restored adobes attract busloads of tourists. They march through the reconstructed plaza which was once the stomping ground of outlaws and desperadoes, including Billy-the-Kid, Butch Hubert, and such politicians and lawmen as Judge Albert Fountain and Pat Garrett.

The fertile Mesilla Valley supplies a host of fresh vegetables year 'round, including zucchini, lettuce, eggplant, black-eyed peas, and various varieties of beans, as well as peppers of all types. The cantaloupes grown here are the sweetest, and the area boasts one of the largest pecan orchards in the world.

Zesty Pecan Balls

¾ lb. CHEDDAR CHEESE
1 pkg. (8 oz.) CREAM
  CHEESE

8 oz. chopped GREEN
  CHILE
1 cup PECANS

Finely grate cheddar cheese and mix with cream cheese. Mix in green chile and form into bite-size balls. Finely grind the pecans, roll the balls in nuts, chill until firm and serve.

Approx. 2 dozen balls.

Ensalada de Col #1
(New Mexican Cole Slaw)

Cole slaw is the perfect accompaniment to many New Mexican dishes.

1 med.-size head CABBAGE,
  shredded
½ med.-size white or yellow
  ONION, finely-chopped
¼ cup SALAD OIL
2 Tbsp. RED WINE
  VINEGAR

1 Tbsp. LEMON JUICE
½ tsp. SALT
½ tsp. CELERY SALT
½ tsp. GARLIC SALT
½ tsp. ground BLACK
  PEPPER

Mix cabbage and onion together in a bowl. Mix rest of ingredients together, pour over cabbage, toss lightly and serve.

Serves 6 to 8.

Ensalada de Col #2
(Cole Slaw)

1 med.-size head CABBAGE coarsely-grated
½ med.-size white or yellow ONION, finely-chopped
2 Tbsp. SOUR CREAM
2 Tbsp. MAYONNAISE
1 tsp. RED WINE VINEGAR
1 tsp. LEMON JUICE
½ tsp. SALT
½ tsp. CELERY SALT
½ tsp. GARLIC SALT
½ tsp. ground BLACK PEPPER

Mix cabbage and onion together in a bowl. Mix rest of ingredients together and lightly toss with cabbage.

Serves 6 to 8.

TIP: *Jicama, a Mexican vegetable, is very popular in New Mexico as well. Peel the rough light brown skin away from this tuber and you have a taste that is somewhere between a radish and a Jerusalem artichoke. Slice the jicama, julienne, and serve in salads, on relish trays, or with dips.*

Eggplant/Chile Casserole

1 med.-size EGGPLANT
½ lb. BUTTER
2 med.-size white ONIONS, peeled and thinly-sliced
4 med.-size TOMATOES, peeled and sliced
½ cup chopped GREEN CHILE (fresh or canned)
1 cup grated PROVOLONE CHEESE*

½ tsp. pressed GARLIC
½ tsp. ground WHITE PEPPER
½ tsp. PAPRIKA
½ tsp. CELERY SALT
1 cup BREAD CRUMBS
2 Tbsp. PARMESAN CHEESE

Slice eggplant into half-inch-thick slices and peel off skin. Put eggplant in a large bowl of cold water with two tablespoons salt. Weight with a plate and let stand for 30 minutes. Remove, rinse well, and lay slices on paper towels, again weighting down with plates until all moisture is absorbed.

Then cut eggplant in half-inch cubes. Melt half the butter in a frying pan and saute eggplant for five minutes, then layer in a well-buttered casserole dish with alternate layers of onion slices, tomato slices, green chile and grated cheese. Mix all spices together and sprinkle a little over each layer as you go.

Top off with bread crumbs mixed with Parmesan cheese, dot with remaining butter and bake in a 350-degree oven for 45 minutes, or until nicely browned.   Serves 4.

*If you want to make it more "American," you can substitute American cheese for the Provolone cheese.

Baked Okra and Rice with Green Chile

2 cups sliced OKRA
½ cup uncooked white RICE
1 cup COLD WATER
½ tsp. SALT

2 Tbsp. BUTTER
½ cup chopped GREEN
   CHILE (fresh or canned)
1 cup TOMATO SAUCE

Remove stem ends and tips of okra pods and cut into half-inch slices to make two cups. Put in a saucepan, add rice, water, salt and green chile, and cook, covered, over low heat for 30 minutes. Pour mixture into a well-greased baking dish and add tomato sauce. Bake for 10 minutes in 375-degree oven.

Serves 4.

Hatch-Stuffed Potatoes

4 large white POTATOES
2 Tbsp. chopped GREEN
   CHILE (fresh or canned)
4 Tbsp. BUTTER
¼ cup HEAVY CREAM

¼ cup dry (French)
   VERMOUTH
1 Tbsp. finely-chopped
   fresh PARSLEY
PAPRIKA

Bake potatoes until just done. Remove from oven and cut each in half the long way. Scoop out pulp and mash with remaining ingredients. Spoon back into shells, sprinkle with paprika and bake in 400-degree oven for 30 minutes.

Serves 4.

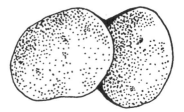

Zucchini Pancakes

2 EGG YOLKS
½ cup all-purpose FLOUR
½ tsp. SALT
¼ tsp. ground BLACK
  PEPPER

2 Tbsp. chopped GREEN
  CHILE (fresh or canned)
2 cups shredded ZUCCHINI
2 EGG WHITES
OIL for frying

Beat egg yolks and combine with flour, salt and pepper. Stir in green chile and then mix in zucchini. Beat egg whites until stiff and fold into zucchini mixture. Heat one inch of oil until hot and drop mixture by the tablespoon into oil and brown on both sides.   Serves 4.

Enchiladas Coloradas
(Red Enchiladas)

2 cups RED CHILE SAUCE (see recipe)
2 Tbsp. COOKING OIL
12 CORN TORTILLAS
½ lb. grated LONGHORN CHEESE

1 large white or yellow ONION, finely-chopped
1 Tbsp. BUTTER
4 EGGS
shredded LETTUCE

Heat chile sauce over low heat. While it is heating through, heat the oil in a frying pan. Using tongs, dip each tortilla in the hot oil just long enough to soften it. DO NOT FRY! Place tortillas, one at a time, on oven-proof plate, spoon on one or two tablespoons of red chile sauce, sprinkle with cheese and onion, and repeat the process with two more tortillas. Put plate in a warm oven to melt cheese and repeat the procedure until all four plates are in oven.

Melt butter in a frying pan and fry eggs the way you like them (over-easy works best for this dish). Place one egg on top of each enchilada plate. Decorate edges of plate with shredded lettuce and serve.   Serves 4.

Green Enchilada Casserole

No pot luck supper in the Mesilla Valley is considered complete without at least one Green Enchilada Casserole.

2 Tbsp. COOKING OIL
  (or bacon drippings)
12 CORN TORTILLAS
½ cup yellow ONION,
  finely-chopped
1 cup, plus ¼ cup grated
  LONGHORN CHEESE
1 can (10¾ oz.) condensed
  CREAM of ASPARAGUS
  SOUP

1 can (10¾ oz.) condensed
  CREAM of CELERY SOUP
¼ cup CREAM
4 oz. chopped GREEN
  CHILE (fresh or canned)
½ tsp. SALT
½ tsp. ground BLACK
  PEPPER
½ tsp. GARLIC SALT

Heat oil in a frying pan or cast-iron skillet. Using tongs, dip each tortilla in the hot oil just long enough to soften it. Alternate tortillas with chopped onion and cup of grated cheese in a casserole dish. Mix soups, cream and chile together and heat in a saucepan. Stir in salt, pepper and garlic salt, and pour over tortillas. Sprinkle one-fourth cup cheese over top and bake in a 325-degree oven for 30 minutes, or until hot and bubbly.

Serves 4 to 6.

Spinach Noodles with Green Chile Sauce

Makes an excellent side dish with pork chops or veal.

1 lb. SPINACH NOODLES
¼ lb. BUTTER
6 cloves GARLIC, cut in half

½ cup chopped GREEN
  CHILE (fresh or canned)

Cook noodles according to package directions. While they are cooking, melt butter and stir in garlic and chile. Drain noodles, pour into a serving bowl, and toss lightly with butter mixture.

Serves 4 to 6.

Red Chile Stew

A dish that has many variations. Here is the one that I got good reviews on when I served it to my customers in my different restaurants.

2 Tbsp. COOKING OIL
2 med.-size yellow or white ONIONS, coarsely-chopped
4 cloves GARLIC
2 lbs. lean STEWING BEEF (or cubed PORK)
2 Tbsp. RED CHILE POWDER
1 Tbsp. BLACK PEPPER
1 Tbsp. dried PARSLEY
¼ cup RED WINE
WATER to cover
3 med.-size WHITE POTATOES, peeled and cut into bite-size pieces

Heat oil in a large pan or Dutch oven. Saute onions in oil until they are transparent. Run garlic through a garlic press and add to onions. Cut meat into bite-size pieces and saute with onions until it is brown. Add chile powder, pepper, parsley, wine and water. Simmer for three hours, or until beef is just getting tender. Add potatoes and simmer for another 45 minutes, or until both the meat and potatoes are done and tender.

Serves 4 to 6.

Salsa Picante
(New Mexican Hot Sauce)

12 JALAPEÑO PEPPERS	2 med.-size white or yellow
3 large green BELL	ONIONS, coarsely-
PEPPERS	chopped
1 can (15 oz.) whole peeled	2 tsp. GARLIC SALT
TOMATOES	1 tsp. ground WHITE
(reserve liquid)	PEPPER

Remove stems and seeds from jalapeños. Run peppers, tomatoes and onions through food processor or blender, and grind coarsely. Stir in garlic salt and pepper, and serve with tortilla chips. (To make a thinner sauce, add reserved juice from tomatoes.) Makes approx. 2 cups.

New Mexico Chicken with Rice

1 cup COOKING OIL
2 cloves GARLIC, peeled,
  sliced in half
1 med.-size frying CHICKEN,
  cut into serving pieces
½ cup long grain white RICE
1 cup WATER
1 btl. or can (12 oz.) BEER
1 tsp. ground CUMIN
1 tsp. SAFFLOWER

1 tsp. ground BLACK
  PEPPER
1 tsp. dried PARSLEY
1 pkg. frozen GREEN PEAS
1 Tbsp. BUTTER
1 tsp. ground BLACK
  PEPPER
1 small jar chopped
  PIMIENTOS

Heat half of the oil in a large pan or Dutch oven, and cook garlic for two minutes. Add chicken pieces and brown well on all sides. Remove and set aside.

Add rest of oil to pan, stir in rice, water, beer, cumin, safflower, pepper and parsley. Return chicken to pan and cook, covered, over low heat until rice is done and chicken is tender (about one hour).

Cook peas according to package directions, and drain. Stir butter, pepper and pimientos into peas. Put chicken and rice in center of a platter. Arrange peas around the rice and serve.

Serves 4.

New Mexico Pot Roast

3 to 3½ lb. boneless
CHUCK ROAST
½ cup all-purpose FLOUR
1 tsp. PAPRIKA
½ tsp. ground BLACK
PEPPER
1 tsp. GARLIC SALT
1 tsp. RED CHILE POWDER
2 Tbsp. BUTTER

1 cup WATER
1 cup dry RED WINE
4 oz. chopped GREEN
CHILE (fresh or canned)
1 clove GARLIC, peeled,
cut in half
2 BAY LEAVES,
broken in half
1 tsp. RED CHILE POWDER

Rinse meat and pat dry with paper towel. Mix flour, paprika, pepper, garlic salt and red chile powder in a plastic or paper bag. Shake meat in the bag to coat it. Melt butter in a Dutch oven or oven-proof dish.

Sear roast on all sides over high heat. Remove from heat, add water, wine, green chile, garlic, bay leaves and red chile powder.

Cover and bake in 350-degree oven for 2½ to 3 hours, or until meat tests very tender. Remove bay leaves before serving.

Serves 4 to 6.

Chile Rellenos
(Stuffed Green Chile)

8 fresh GREEN CHILES
1 cup grated LONGHORN
  (or Velveeta®) CHEESE
½ cup all-purpose FLOUR
1 tsp. PAPRIKA
½ tsp. GARLIC SALT
½ tsp. BAKING POWDER
2 EGGS, well-beaten
1 cup COOKING OIL

Roast and peel chiles, cut off top of pod and remove seeds. (A boning knife works well for this job.) Divide cheese equally among chiles and fill each chile with cheese (you can fill them either through the top or cut a slit down the center).

Mix flour, paprika, garlic salt and baking powder together, and roll each chile in the flour mixture. Dip chiles in beaten egg, then again in flour mixture, then egg. Refrigerate for 15 minutes.

Heat oil and fry chile in hot oil until golden brown. Place in an oven-proof serving dish and keep in a warm oven until all the chiles are done.   Serves 4.

Green Tomato Mincemeat

6 cups tart APPLES,
  peeled and chopped
4 cups coarsely-chopped
  GREEN TOMATOES
4 tsp. ground CINNAMON
2 tsp. SALT
2 tsp. ground ALLSPICE
2 tsp. ground CLOVES
1 cup coarsely-ground
  SEEDLESS RAISINS
2½ cups SUGAR

Mix all ingredients together and cook over medium heat for about one hour, then turn up heat and bring to a boil. Simmer until thick. Pour into prepared hot sterilized canning jars, leaving one inch head space and seal as soon as cool. Place in freezer. Will keep up to three months.   Yield: 5 pints.

Green Chile Jelly

Great with cream cheese on crackers!

4 whole GREEN CHILES
4 large GREEN BELL
  PEPPERS
1 cup white distilled
  VINEGAR

5 cups SUGAR
1 bottle (6 oz.) liquid
  FRUIT PECTIN

Roast, peel and remove seeds from chiles. (Can use canned.) Core, remove stems and seeds from peppers. Coarsely-chop peppers and run through a food processor with chiles. Bring to a boil in a large pot with vinegar and sugar, and cook for 30 minutes, or until mixture is transparent. Remove from heat and let cool for 10 to 15 minutes, then stir pectin into mixture. Pour into sterilized jars and seal with paraffin.

Makes 4 half-pint jars.

Sopaipillas

2 cups FLOUR
2 tsp. BAKING POWDER
1 level tsp. SALT
1 tsp. SUGAR

1 Tbsp. pure LARD
  (or shortening)
WARM WATER
OIL for deep-fat frying
HONEY

Mix flour with baking powder, salt and sugar. Cut lard (or shortening) into flour mixture. Add enough warm water to make a medium-soft dough similar to a pie crust. Put dough in a covered bowl and let stand at room temperature for 30 minutes. Then roll dough on floured board to 1/8-inch thickness. Cut into three-inch triangles and fry in deep hot fat until sopaipillas are fluffy and golden brown. Remove from fat and drain on paper towels. Serve hot with honey.

Makes 2 dozen.

Deep Dish Pecan Pie

5 EGGS
1 cup light CORN SYRUP
1 cup MAPLE SYRUP
¼ tsp. SALT
1 tsp. VANILLA

¼ cup all-purpose FLOUR
2 Tbsp. melted BUTTER
9-inch unbaked deep dish
　PIE SHELL
1 cup coarsely-chopped
　PECANS

Preheat oven to 425 degrees.

Beat the eggs well. Add remaining ingredients EXCEPT THE PECANS, and beat. Pour mixture into unbaked pie shell. Sprinkle pecans over top of mixture, and thump pecans with a fork so they are covered with the liquid. Bake at 425 degrees for 15 minutes, reduce heat to 350 degrees and bake for another 30 minutes or until filling is set.　　　　　Serves 6 to 8.

Empanadas
(Fruit Turnovers)

For the Dough:

2 cups all-purpose FLOUR	MILK
1 tsp. SALT	COOKING OIL
2 tsp. BAKING POWDER	POWDERED SUGAR
2 Tbsp. BUTTER (or lard)	VANILLA ICE CREAM

Combine flour, salt and baking powder. Cut butter into flour until well mixed. Carefully add enough milk to make a dough of medium consistency. Roll out dough very thin. Cut into circles, about 3 to 3½ inches in diameter.

The Filling:

½ cup MINCEMEAT combined with 1 Tbsp. BRANDY

or

½ cup APRICOT PRESERVES mixed with 1 Tbsp. BRANDY

or

½ cup PEACH PRESERVES mixed with 1 Tbsp. BRANDY

Spoon a teaspoon of filling into each circle, fold in half and pinch the semicircle edges together. Heat oil and fry in very hot oil until golden brown. Sprinkle with powdered sugar and serve warm with vanilla ice cream.

Makes approx. one dozen empanadas.

Orange Biscochitos

Some folks call them Biscochos, some call them Biscochitos. There was even a hot debate in the New Mexico State Legislature during the 1980s on the correct spelling and whether this delicious cookie should be designated as the "state cookie." Here is my version:

1½ cups LARD
1 cup plus ½ Tbsp. SUGAR
6 EGG YOLKS
½ cup undiluted FROZEN
   ORANGE JUICE
1 Tbsp. TRIPLE SEC

3½ tsp. BAKING POWDER
2 tsp. ANISE SEEDS
5 to 5½ cups all-purpose
   FLOUR
1 Tbsp. plus pinch
   CINNAMON

Cream lard and cup of sugar together until light and fluffy. Beat egg yolks. Beat orange juice and Triple Sec into egg yolks. Then beat in lard and sugar. Add baking powder, anise seeds, flour and pinch of cinnamon and mix thoroughly. Knead the dough and roll very thin. Cut into diamond shapes. Combine tablespoon of cinnamon and one-half tablespoon sugar together, and dip the cookie into the mixture. Place on lightly-greased cookie sheet and bake at 350 degrees for 10 minutes, or until done.   Makes approx. five dozen.

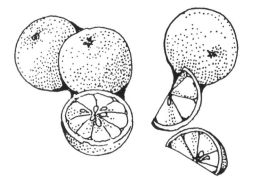

Holiday Sugared Pecans

1 cup WATER
1 lb. SUGAR
1/8 tsp. SALT

1 Tbsp. CREAM SHERRY
1 lb. whole PECANS

Bring water and sugar to a boil and cook until it forms a thick syrup. Add salt and sherry and stir. Stir in the nuts and keep stirring until syrup sugars. Let cool and then separate the nuts. May be stored in a jar until ready to serve.

Midas Touch Pie

1 can (14 oz.) SWEETENED
   CONDENSED MILK
1/3 cup fresh LEMON
   JUICE
1 can (8 oz.) CRUSHED
   PINEAPPLE, drained
1 cup chopped PECANS

1½ cups WHIPPING CREAM
2 Tbsp. SUGAR
1 Tbsp. BRANDY
8-inch graham cracker
   PIE CRUST

Mix together milk, lemon juice, pineapple and pecans. Beat the cream. Halfway through add sugar and brandy. Continue beating until it forms stiff peaks. Fold the whipped cream into the pineapple-pecan mixture. Pour into the crust and chill for at least two hours before serving.   Serves 6 to 8.

West Mesa Pecan Cake

6 EGGS, well beaten
½ lb. BUTTER
2 cups SUGAR
¾ cup MILK
¼ cup BOURBON

4 cups all-purpose FLOUR
4 tsp. BAKING POWDER
pinch of SALT
1 cup SEEDLESS RAISINS
2 cups chopped PECANS

Cream eggs, butter, sugar, milk and bourbon together. Sift flour, baking powder and salt together. Beat the batter, add raisins and pecans. Pour into a bundt pan and bake in a 350-degree oven for one hour, or until done.

Serves 10 to 12.

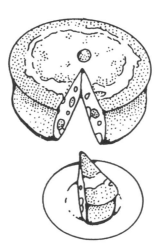

CHAPTER FIVE

The Sophisticated Art of Cooking in the Capital City of Santa Fe

The question is often asked about Santa Fe "What can you say about a town that has everything?" It is beautiful, has great architecture, museums, theatres, nationally-known opera company and civic pride in abundance.

It also boasts a diverse population, some of whom are truly magic people, good restaurants, clean air, a past worth exploring and preserving, a present worth living in, and a future worth looking forward to.

Does it sound like I'm prejudiced? You bet your boots, I am! I've lived in a lot of places—some I like, but I love Santa Fe!

They say, the people that say that sort of thing, that you either fall in love with Santa Fe on the spot or you just shrug your shoulders—unable to see what all the fuss is about—and leave, never to return.

It calls itself the "City Different." And it is! The difference is not just in its architectural code which creates a pleasing uniformity among the buildings, both public and private, but in its people.

Rarely have I encountered people so fiercely proud of their city. Whether native born or adopted, it's the same.

Santa Fe celebrates the individual, revels in characters, loves the wealthy (especially if they show a disdain for their own worldly goods). Someone once remarked to me that there were more Mercedes on the streets of Santa Fe per capita than in either Los Angeles or Berlin, and that most of them had never been washed.

I don't really know how accurate that is, but I do know that there is a feeling about Santa Fe that captures you and if you are "simpatico," it never leaves you.

The Dandy Cocktail

Although I subscribe to Dorothy Parker's dictum that liquor's quicker—with this drink you can have your candy, too!

2 oz. BOURBON
1 tsp. GINGER BRANDY
1 tsp. LIGHT RUM
juice of ¼ LIME

1 stick of ROCK CANDY
GINGER ALE
MINT

Pour bourbon, brandy, rum and lime juice over ice in a tall highball glass. Fill the glass with ginger ale, stir with the rock candy stick and leave it in the glass. Add a sprig of mint and serve.   Makes one drink.

Santa Fe Roses

Cocktail parties never end in Santa Fe. Here is a popular appetizer.

1 cup PECANS
1 clove GARLIC
1 pkg. (6 oz.) CREAM CHEESE
   at room temperature

1 tsp. WORCESTERSHIRE
   SAUCE
2 Tbsp. RED CHILE POWDER

Grind pecans very fine. Mince garlic clove and blend with pecans, cream cheese and the Worcestershire sauce. Shape into small bite-size balls and roll each in the chile powder to coat them. Place on a serving plate and chill until firm. Serve garnished with fresh parsley. Makes approx. two dozen balls.

Chicken Liver Paté a la Canyon Road

1 lb. CHICKEN LIVERS
1 cup BUTTER
¼ cup chopped fresh
   CILANTRO
1/3 cup white TEQUILA

¼ tsp. GARLIC SALT
¼ tsp. ground WHITE
   PEPPER
2 med.-size GREEN ONIONS,
   chopped

Wash chicken livers well and pat dry on paper towels. Melt butter in a frying pan and saute chicken livers in butter until they are just cooked through. Do not overcook, or they will be tough.

Let cool and put livers into a blender. Add cilantro, tequila, garlic salt, pepper and green onions. Blend until smooth. Refrigerate for at least six hours. Serve with crackers.

Makes one pound of pate.

Rolled Watercress Sandwiches

1 bunch WATERCRESS,
   washed and patted dry
   (Save 12 pieces of watercress for garnish)
¼ tsp. GARLIC SALT

3 oz. CREAM CHEESE
   at room temperature
12 slices very thin
   WHITE BREAD

Chop watercress and mix with garlic salt and cream cheese. Remove crusts from bread and roll bread slices as thin as possible with a rolling pin, but do not tear them. Spread each slice with a layer of the mixture. Roll up like a jelly roll. Put a piece of watercress into the end of each roll. Chill and serve.

Yield: 12 sandwiches.

Crab Puffs

8 oz. cooked CRAB MEAT
2 GREEN ONIONS,
  chopped finely
½ cup CHEDDAR CHEESE,
  grated
1 tsp. WORCESTERSHIRE
  SAUCE
½ tsp. DRY MUSTARD
1 cup WATER
½ cup BUTTER
⅛ tsp. SALT
⅛ tsp. GARLIC POWDER
1 cup all-purpose FLOUR
4 EGGS

Mix together crab, onions, cheese, Worcestershire sauce and mustard. Combine water, butter, salt and garlic powder in a saucepan. Bring to a boil, then remove from heat. Stir in flour with a wire whisk and beat until it forms a ball. Add eggs, one at a time, beating very well after adding each egg.

Stir into crab mixture. Drop by teaspoon onto lightly-buttered baking sheet. Bake in 400-degree oven for 15 minutes. Reduce heat to 350 degrees and bake for another 10 minutes, or until lightly browned. Serve hot.   Makes approx. 4 dozen.

Shrimp Paté

¼ lb. BUTTER
  (room temperature)
1½ tsp. DIJON MUSTARD
¼ cup very DRY SHERRY
2 Tbsp. fresh LEMON JUICE
¼ tsp. ground MACE
¼ tsp. CAYENNE PEPPER
1 lb. shelled, cooked,
  deveined SHRIMP
  (This is a great way to
  use small, irregular
  shrimp)

Put everything but the shrimp in a blender and mix together. Add shrimp, a few at a time and blend until it makes a paste. Pour into a bowl and refrigerate for at least five hours.

Makes approx. one cup.

Dilly Shrimp

½ cup all-purpose FLOUR
½ tsp. ground WHITE
  PEPPER
1 Tbsp. dried DILL
2 doz. jumbo SHRIMP
  (Shell and devein shrimp.*
  Wash in cold water.)

1 cup MILK
½ lb. BUTTER
4 Tbsp. BUTTER
1 Tbsp. fresh DILL
LEMON SLICES
DRIED PARSLEY

Put flour and pepper in a plastic bag. Crumble dried dill in your fingers and add to bag. Dip shrimp in milk and shake the shrimp in bag to coat.

Melt half-pound of butter in a large frying pan and saute shrimp over moderate heat for five minutes, or until they just turn pink. Transfer to a warm platter and keep warm.

Add four tablespoons butter and fresh dill to the pan and heat very quickly until butter starts to turn brown. Pour over shrimp and serve with lemon slices that have been sprinkled with dried parsley.   Serves 4.

*There is a marvelous, inexpensive plastic gadget (for sale in many supermarkets) that makes deveining and shelling shrimp very easy.

Stuffed Ripe Olives

1 can ripe, pitted OLIVES
¼ cup OLIVE OIL
1 Tbsp. RED WINE
   VINEGAR
1 tsp. RED CHILE POWDER

¼ tsp. DRIED OREGANO
2 cloves GARLIC
¼ cup DRY VERMOUTH
   (French)
Strips of GREEN CHILE

Drain the olives and put into a bowl. Mix the oil, vinegar, chile powder and oregano together and pour over olives. Run garlic through a garlic press and stir into mixture. Add vermouth and stir. Cover and marinate in refrigerator for at least 24 hours.

Cut green chile into pieces small enough to fit inside each olive. Stuff each olive with a piece of green chile and secure with a toothpick. Serve.

Homemade Corn Chips

3 cups CORN FLOUR
   (masa harina)
¾ tsp. SALT

½ tsp. CUMIN
1½ cups WATER
OIL for deep frying

Combine corn flour, salt and cumin in a large mixing bowl. Gently stir in water until it forms a dough. Divide into 14 portions and form each into a ball. Place each ball between plastic wrap and roll in a circle about six inches in diameter. Cut each circle into six pie-shaped pieces with a pizza cutter.

Pour oil in a deep fat fryer or a large cast-iron Dutch oven. Heat to 375 degrees and fry chips, in small batches, until nice and brown. Drain on paper towels. Add salt if desired.

Makes approx. 9 dozen chips.

TIP: *Keep masa harina or corn meal in the freezer to keep it fresh and bug free.*

Sweet Potato Chips

Large SWEET POTATOES
OIL for deep frying
SALT

Peel sweet potatoes and slice as thin as possible. Let slices stand in cold water for two hours. Dry well and fry a few at a time in oil heated to 375 degrees, until they are a golden brown.

Scallop Salad

½ cup dry WHITE WINE
½ cup WATER
4 sprigs fresh PARSLEY
⅛ tsp. TARRAGON

1 med.-size WHITE
   ONION
1½ lbs. bay SCALLOPS

Combine the wine, water, parsley and tarragon in a saucepan. Chop onion and add. Bring to a boil, then add scallops and simmer for three minutes or until done. Let cool, then drain.

1 cup sliced white
   MUSHROOMS
10 slices, pitted
   GREEN OLIVES
2 tsp. chopped
   GREEN CHILE

1 Tbsp. MAYONNAISE
1 tsp. prepared ITALIAN
   DRESSING
LETTUCE
CHERRY TOMATOES
RADISHES

Mix together and toss lightly with the scallops. Serve on a bed of leaf lettuce. Garnish with slices of mushroom, olives and roses made from cherry tomatoes and radishes.

Serves 4.

Watercress and Orange Salad with Pecan-Chile Dressing

2 bunches WATERCRESS
3 med.-size ORANGES

Wash watercress well, cut off very bottom stems and dry well. Peel oranges and section. (Remove seeds if not seedless oranges.) Chill oranges for 30 minutes in refrigerator, then combine with watercress in a salad bowl. Dress with the following dressing.   Serves 6.

Pecan-Chile Dressing

½ cup PEANUT OIL
2 Tbsp. virgin OLIVE OIL
2 Tbsp. LEMON JUICE
1 Tbsp. HONEY

juice of 1 ORANGE
2 Tbsp. chopped GREEN
   CHILE (fresh or canned)
½ cup chopped PECANS

Put everything but the pecans in a blender and blend well. Then add pecans and chill until ready to dress the salad.

Sweet and Sour Cucumbers

3 med.-size CUCUMBERS
1 med.-size RED ONION
¼ cup SOUR CREAM
2 Tbsp. HONEY

3 Tbsp. GARLIC WINE
   VINEGAR
2 Tbsp. chopped GREEN
   CHILE (fresh or canned)

Peel cucumbers and onion, and slice thinly. Mix together in a salad bowl. Then mix together sour cream, honey, vinegar and green chile. Pour over cucumbers and onions, and refrigerate at least one hour before serving.   Serves 4 to 6.

Creamed Baked Broccoli

This makes a great side dish for roast beef or pork.

1½ qts. chopped, cooked
   BROCCOLI
½ cup MAYONNAISE
½ cup BUTTER

2 tsp. LEMON JUICE
½ cup chopped GREEN
   CHILE (fresh or canned)
¼ tsp. NUTMEG

Cook broccoli, drain. Mix remaining ingredients together and add to broccoli. Pour into a lightly-buttered casserole or baking dish, sprinkle nutmeg over top and bake in a 325-degree oven until hot and bubbly.   Serves 4 to 6.

Ham & Chile Mousse

2 cups diced, cooked HAM
½ cup diced GREEN CHILE
2 EGG YOLKS
¼ tsp. ground NUTMEG
½ tsp. Dijon-style MUSTARD

⅛ tsp. GROUND CLOVES
1 cup HEAVY CREAM
2 Tbsp. DRY SHERRY
¼ tsp. TABASCO® SAUCE
2 EGG WHITES

Run diced ham through finest blade of a food processor or chopper. Stir in chile. Beat egg yolks, add to ham mixture along with the nutmeg, mustard and cloves. Beat cream until just stiff, then stir in sherry and Tabasco®. Fold into ham mixture.

Beat egg whites until stiff and fold into mixture. Spoon into a lightly-buttered souffle dish and bake in a 325-degree oven for one-half hour, or until firm. Serve at once with Hollandaise Sauce.   Serves 4.

Hollandaise Sauce

¼ lb. BUTTER,
   divided in half
2 EGG YOLKS,
   lightly beaten

1 Tbsp. LEMON JUICE
dash of CAYENNE PEPPER

Place half of the butter in a small saucepan with egg yolks and lemon juice in the top of a double boiler over hot (not boiling) water. Stir mixture constantly until butter melts. Add rest of the butter and continue stirring until mixture thickens. Remove from top of double boiler and stir in cayenne pepper. Serve at once.   Yield: Approx. one-half cup.

Crab Meat Enchiladas
(With Tomatillo Sauce)

2 Tbsp. BUTTER
12 oz. CRAB MEAT
2 cloves GARLIC

1 tsp. PARSLEY
4 large FLOUR
TORTILLAS

Melt butter in a frying pan and stir in crab meat. Peel garlic cloves, mince and stir into crab. Add parsley and cook until crab meat is just warmed through. Heat tortillas until just warm and place flat on each plate. Put three ounces of crab meat mixture in center of each tortilla and fold over. Pour tomatillo sauce over them and serve immediately. Serves 4.

Tomatillo Sauce

2 Tbsp. PEANUT OIL
1 med.-size WHITE ONION
1 lb. fresh TOMATILLOS
1 med.-size GREEN BELL
    PEPPER
½ cup dry WHITE WINE
    (or dry vermouth)

1 cup CHICKEN STOCK
2 oz. chopped GREEN
    CHILE (fresh or canned)
½ tsp. GARLIC SALT
½ tsp. GARLIC POWDER
¼ tsp. ground BLACK
    PEPPER

Heat peanut oil in a frying pan. Peel and finely chop onion and saute in oil until it is transparent. Peel tomatillos, remove stems, dice well and add to pan. Remove stem, seeds and core green pepper, dice and add to the pan. Add wine, chicken stock, chile and seasonings.

Simmer over low heat until tomatillos are soft. Pour over crab meat enchiladas.

Julian's Special Haddock

1 large white ONION
2 Tbsp. COOKING OIL
1 cup TOMATO SAUCE
3 tsp. CAPERS
½ cup sliced, STUFFED
  OLIVES
¼ cup chopped GREEN
  CHILE (fresh or canned)
2 cups CRACKER CRUMBS
2 lbs. HADDOCK FILLETS
BUTTER
PAPRIKA

Chop onion and saute it in the oil. Remove onion with a slotted spoon and mix with tomato sauce, capers, olives and chile. Sprinkle one cup of cracker crumbs on the bottom of a 9 x 13" baking dish. Put haddock on top of crumbs, and pour tomato mixture over them. Sprinkle remaining crumbs on top, dot with butter and sprinkle with paprika. Bake in 400-degree oven for 20 minutes or until fish is done.   Serves 4.

Rolled Tortillas
with Sour Cream and Cottage Cheese

3 cups SOUR CREAM
2 cups COTTAGE CHEESE
½ tsp. SALT
½ tsp. ground WHITE
    PEPPER
½ cup BUTTER
18 CORN TORTILLAS

1 lb. Monterey Jack
    CHEESE, cut into strips
1½ cups chopped GREEN
    CHILE (fresh or canned)
½ cup grated LONGHORN
    CHEESE

Mix the sour cream, cottage cheese, salt and pepper together. Melt butter in a frying pan and heat tortillas 30 seconds (just until soft) on each side. Divide strips of Monterey Jack and chile on the tortillas and roll them up. Put rolled tortillas in a lightly-buttered, shallow baking dish. Spoon sour cream mixture over them. Sprinkle with grated longhorn cheese and bake in 350-degree oven for 30 minutes, or until very hot. Serves 6.

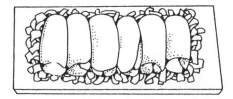

Chorizo-Rice Casserole

1 lb. CHORIZO SAUSAGE
3 cups cold, cooked RICE
2 med.-size ONIONS, chopped
1 med.-size GREEN BELL PEPPER, coarsely-chopped
1 tsp. RED CHILE POWDER
½ lb. CHEDDAR CHEESE, diced
1 can (10 oz.) CREAM-STYLE CORN
1 can (8 oz.) TOMATO SAUCE
¼ cup seedless RAISINS
½ tsp. GARLIC SALT
¼ tsp. ground BLACK PEPPER
6 large GREEN, STUFFED OLIVES
¼ cup DRY RED WINE
6 hard-cooked EGGS, quartered

Crumble chorizo in a frying pan and saute until browned. Mix all other ingredients together (except the eggs) and pour into a well-greased casserole dish. Gently put egg wedges about one-quarter-inch into the mixture. Top with chorizo and bake in 350-degree oven for 30 minutes.   Serves 6.

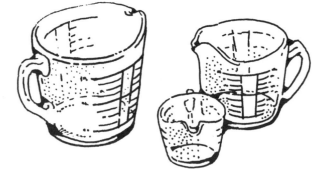

New Mexico Trout in Marinade

Some fine trout are caught in the streams of northern New Mexico and served in Santa Fe restaurants and homes.

4 med.-size TROUT, cleaned
½ cup COOKING OIL
½ cup LEMON JUICE
½ cup DRY VERMOUTH

½ tsp. dried PARSLEY
½ tsp. coarse ground
  BLACK PEPPER
1 Tbsp. SHRIMP BOIL
  (or herb mix for fish)

Wash the trout in cold water and dry on paper towels. Mix rest of ingredients together and marinate trout in mixture for one hour. Remove fish and strain marinade. Broil fish to taste, basting with marinade twice during broiling time.   Serves 4.

Shrimp Don Cubero

1 can (10¾ oz.) condensed
  Cream of ASPARAGUS
  SOUP
1 can (10¾ oz.) condensed
  Cream of CELERY SOUP
½ cup MILK
¼ cup SHERRY
1 med.-size can chopped
  MUSHROOMS

4 oz. chopped GREEN
  CHILE (fresh or canned)
½ tsp. GARLIC SALT
½ tsp. CELERY SALT
1 tsp. dried PARSLEY
½ tsp. ground BLACK
  PEPPER
1 lb. med.-size SHRIMP,
  shelled and deveined

Put soup in a saucepan, add milk and sherry. Drain mushrooms and add to soup along with chile and spices. Cook over low heat until warm. Drain shrimp and rinse under cold water. Gently stir into soup. Cook until hot and serve over toast points or rice.   Serves 4.

Chilled Fish
with Guacamole Sauce

2 lbs. HALIBUT
   FILLETS
½ tsp. SALT
½ tsp. ground WHITE
   PEPPER

1 Tbsp. fresh LEMON JUICE
¼ tsp. THYME
1 BAY LEAF
½ white ONION,
   thinly-sliced

Put fillets in a lightly-buttered baking dish and season with salt and pepper. Sprinkle lemon juice on them, add thyme, bay leaf and sliced onions to pan. Bake in 400-degree oven for 20 minutes, or until fish tests done. When fish is done, let cool, then chill in refrigerator for at least two hours. Remove and discard bay leaf. Serve with Guacamole Sauce.   Serves 4.

Guacamole Sauce

2 good-size AVOCADOS,
   peeled and mashed
1 tsp. fresh LEMON JUICE
¼ small WHITE ONION,
   finely-minced
1 small ripe TOMATO,
   peeled and diced

¼ tsp. TABASCO® SAUCE
¼ tsp. SALT
¼ tsp. ground BLACK
   PEPPER

Mix all ingredients together and serve over Chilled Fish.
      Serves 4.

Oven-Barbecued Short Ribs

2 lbs. BEEF SHORT RIBS
OIL for browning ribs
½ cup RED WINE
8 oz. TOMATO SAUCE
¼ cup yellow ONION,
  finely-chopped
½ tsp. SALT

½ tsp. GARLIC POWDER
1 tsp. dried PARSLEY
  FLAKES
2 Tbsp. LEMON JUICE
1 Tbsp. prepared MUSTARD
1 Tbsp. WORCESTERSHIRE
  SAUCE
2 Tbsp. chopped GREEN
  CHILE (fresh or canned)

Brown ribs on all sides in oil, drain and put into heavy Dutch oven or pan. Combine rest of ingredients and pour over ribs. Cover and bake in 325-degree oven for two hours, or until done.

Serves 4.

Blue Corn Meal Muffins

Friends of ours make these for us every time we visit Santa Fe. I really look forward to them.

1½ cups all-purpose FLOUR
1 cup BLUE CORN MEAL
1 tsp. BAKING POWDER
1 tsp. SALT

1 tsp. SUGAR
1½ cups MILK
1/3 cup COOKING OIL
2 EGGS

Preheat oven to 400 degrees.
Sift flour with corn meal and baking powder. Then mix with salt and sugar. Stir in milk and oil. Beat eggs and stir into mixture. Grease a 12-hole muffin pan. Fill each hole three-fourths full and bake at 400 degrees for 20 to 25 minutes.

Makes 12 muffins.

Mocha Cream Pie

¼ lb. BUTTER,
at room temperature
1½ cups CHOCOLATE
WAFER CRUMBS
12 large WHITE
MARSHMALLOWS

½ cup MILK
8 oz. SEMI-SWEET
CHOCOLATE
¼ cup strong BLACK
COFFEE
2 Tbsp. KAHLUA®
1½ cups heavy CREAM

Combine butter and chocolate crumbs and press evenly into the bottom and sides of an eight-inch pie pan. Stir marshmallows and milk together in a pan over low heat (or microwave). Then let cool to room temperature.

While marshmallow mixture is cooling, melt chocolate in top of double boiler (or microwave), then stir in coffee and liqueur. Pour chocolate into marshmallow mixture.

Whip one cup of cream and fold into mixture, then pour into the crumb crust and refrigerate for two hours. Whip remaining cream to garnish top of pie.   Serves 8.

Coffee 'n' Cream Cheesecake

3 pkgs. (8 oz. each) CREAM
CHEESE, room temp.
1/2 cup SUGAR
2 cups SOUR CREAM
6 Tbsp. all-purpose FLOUR
6 EGGS

3 Tbsp. strong BLACK
COFFEE
1/4 cup KAHLUA®
GRAHAM CRACKER CRUST
CHOCOLATE CURLS

Beat together cream cheese and sugar. Blend in sour cream and flour. Beat eggs and add to mixture. Add coffee and liqueur and pour into a graham cracker crust. Bake in 300-degree oven for one hour.

Remove from oven and let cool four to five hours before serving. Garnish with chocolate curls.   Serves 10 to 12.

Cafe Olé

6 to 8 cups hot BLACK
   COFFEE
3 oz. LIME JUICE

6 tsp. SUGAR
9 oz. gold TEQUILA
WHIPPED CREAM

Mix all ingredients together (except whipped cream). Serve in mugs with a dollop of whipped cream on top.   Serves 6.

CHAPTER SIX

The Duke City

The city of Albuquerque was founded in 1706 by Father Manuel Moreno. He walked more than sixty miles with a band of faithful followers from Santa Fe to the site of what is now known as "old town," Albuquerque, an area that presently hosts hordes of tourists every day.

Fr. Moreno named this new village after his patron, San Francisco de Alburquerque, the Viceroy of Mexico. The Viceroy, knowing which side his political bread was buttered on, ordered the good father to change the name to San Felipe de Alburquerque in honor of Philip V, King of Spain. In time, both the San Felipe and the first "r" in Albuquerque were dropped.

The Duke City has had its share of saints and sinners throughout the years and has grown into a large, thriving city with a great deal of charm and an easy-going southwestern life style.

Spicy Nine-Bean Soup

1/3 cup LENTILS, dried
1/3 cup BABY LIMA BEANS
1/3 cup LIMA BEANS
1/3 cup PINTO BEANS
1/3 cup GREAT NORTHERN
  BEANS
1/3 cup NAVY BEANS
1/3 cup BLACK-EYED
  PEAS
1/3 cup SPLIT PEAS
1/3 cup KIDNEY BEANS
½ cup chopped GREEN
  CHILE (fresh or canned)

2 Tbsp. ground RED CHILE
2 cups diced, cooked HAM
1 med.-size yellow ONION,
  chopped
1 Tbsp. dried PARSLEY
  FLAKES
2 tsp. GARLIC POWDER
2 Tbsp. BACON FAT
2 BEEF BOUILLON CUBES
1 tsp. ground BLACK
  PEPPER
TABASCO® SAUCE
  to taste

Put all beans in a large soup pot, cover with water and bring to a boil. Turn off heat and let set for 45 minutes. Drain, rinse under cold water and put beans into a crock pot.

Add remaining ingredients to crock pot, cover with water and cook on high for one hour. Turn to low and cook for six hours, or until beans are nicely done. Serves 6 to 8.

Sausage, Cabbage and Chile Pie

2 lbs. bulk SAUSAGE
1 cup chopped yellow
ONION
1 med.-size green
CABBAGE
2 cups whole peeled, cooked
TOMATOES, with juice
1 cup chopped GREEN
CHILE (fresh or canned)

½ tsp. dried BASIL
1 tsp. SALT
½ tsp. ground BLACK
PEPPER
1 tsp. TABASCO® SAUCE
2 Tbsp. all-purpose FLOUR
¼ cup COLD WATER
PIE CRUST

Brown sausage and onion together in a large, heavy pot over medium heat. Then drain off any excess fat. Remove core from cabbage and cut cabbage into one-inch pieces, and add to the sausage mixture. Then add tomatoes, chile, basil, salt, pepper and Tabasco®. Cook, covered for 15 minutes over low heat until cabbage is tender.

Mix flour and water together and add to cabbage-sausage mixture and cook until thickened, stirring well. Pour mixture into a two-quart casserole dish. Top with pie crust and bake in 350-degree oven until pastry is lightly brown.

Serves 6.

Meatless Stuffed Peppers

3 large GREEN BELL
  PEPPERS
3 Tbsp. BUTTER
1 cup diced ONION
½ lb. fresh MUSHROOMS,
  cleaned and chopped
3 Tbsp. chopped GREEN
  CHILE (fresh or canned)

1 cup RICE, cooked
¼ tsp. ground BLACK
  PEPPER
2 EGGS, lightly-beaten
1 cup RED WINE
½ cup SOUR CREAM

Cut peppers in half lengthwise, remove stems, fibers and seeds. Parboil halves for five minutes, drain and reserve.

Melt butter in a frying pan and brown onions and mushrooms, then stir in rice, green chile and black pepper. Remove from heat and mix with eggs.

Stuff each pepper half and place them in a lightly-buttered baking dish. Pour wine in bottom of dish and baste two or three times while baking the peppers for 45 minutes in a 350-degree oven.

When peppers are tender, remove to a serving platter. Stir sour cream into the remaining liquid in the pan. Pour over peppers and serve.

Serves 6 light eaters or 3 hearty appetites.

Duke City Turkey Salad

2 cups bite-size pieces
COOKED TURKEY
1 cup bite-size pieces
GREEN APPLE
½ cup chopped CELERY
½ cup chopped PECANS
2 Tbsp. MAYONNAISE
1 Tbsp. SOUR CREAM

1 Tbsp. RED CHILE
POWDER
½ tsp. CELERY SALT
¼ tsp. SALT
½ tsp. ground BLACK
PEPPER
¼ tsp. GARLIC POWDER

Mix all ingredients in a bowl and serve on a bed of lettuce leaves arranged on salad plates.   Serves 4.

Lima Bean Salad

1 pkg. (10 oz.) frozen
LIMA BEANS
1 Tbsp. RED WINE
VINEGAR
3 Tbsp. OLIVE OIL
1 Tbsp. DRY VERMOUTH
¼ cup chopped GREEN
CHILE (fresh or canned)
¼ cup finely-chopped
CELERY

¼ cup sweet PICKLE
RELISH
¼ cup sliced pimiento-
stuffed GREEN OLIVES
¼ cup sliced BLACK OLIVES
½ tsp. SALT
½ tsp. ground BLACK
PEPPER

Cook lima beans according to package directions. Drain and put into a salad bowl. Add remaining ingredients and chill in refrigerator at least two hours before serving.   Serves 4.

Corn Souffle

¼ cup BUTTER
¼ cup all-purpose FLOUR
1½ tsp. SALT
1 Tbsp. SUGAR
1¾ cups MILK

3 cups fresh (or frozen)
   CORN, chopped
1 tsp. CAYENNE PEPPER
½ cup chopped GREEN
   CHILE (fresh or canned)
6 EGGS, separated

Melt butter in a saucepan, stir in flour, salt and sugar. Cook until it starts to bubble, then add milk and cook over low heat until it thickens. Stir in corn, remove from heat and let cool. Stir in cayenne pepper and chile. Beat egg yolks and stir into mixture. Beat egg whites until stiff and fold into mixture. Pour into a lightly-buttered souffle dish and bake in a 350-degree oven for 45 minutes, or until done. Serve immediately.

Serves 8.

Pork Chop Casserole

1½ Tbsp. BACON DRIPPINGS
6 good-size PORK CHOPS
1 can creamed-style CORN
1/3 cup chopped GREEN
   CHILE (fresh or canned)

1 tsp. SALT
1 tsp. ground BLACK
   PEPPER
¼ cup HOT WATER

Heat bacon drippings in a skillet, brown pork chops on both sides and put into a lightly-buttered casserole dish. Mix corn, chile, salt, pepper and water together and pour over pork chops.

Cover and bake in 350-degree oven for 30 minutes. Remove cover and bake for 15 more minutes or until done.

Serves 4 to 6.

Ravioli with Pecan Sauce

Make your favorite cheese or meat ravioli or buy the frozen, and use this sauce for a delightful change from the standard tomato or garlic and butter sauces.

Pecan Sauce

¼ lb. BUTTER
1 cup finely-chopped
   PECANS
2 GARLIC cloves (run
   through a garlic press)

2 Tbsp. OLIVE OIL
1 med.-size PIMENTO
   or red BELL PEPPER,
   chopped

Melt the butter in a frying pan. Add remaining ingredients. Cook over low heat until peppers are soft. Serve over ravioli.

Serves 6.

Baked Halibut a la Orlin

4 HALIBUT STEAKS
   (each weighing
   approx. ½ lb.)
2 Tbsp. melted BUTTER
½ cup TOMATOES
½ cup chopped GREEN
   ONIONS

¼ tsp. ground WHITE
   PEPPER
¼ tsp. PAPRIKA
¼ cup dry WHITE
   WINE
¼ cup chopped GREEN
   CHILE (fresh or canned)

Rinse halibut steaks and put into a baking pan. Pour melted butter over them and sprinkle with paprika. Combine remaining ingredients and pour over fish.

Bake in 375-degree oven for 10 minutes. Baste with the liquid and bake for another 20 minutes or until fish is done.

Serves 4.

Cheese Rarebit
with Chile and Beer

1 lb. AMERICAN CHEESE,
   diced
1 Tbsp. BUTTER

1 can (12 oz.) BEER
½ cup chopped GREEN
   CHILE (fresh or canned)
¼ tsp. CAYENNE PEPPER

Melt butter in a heavy pan, add cheese a little at a time and stir until it melts. Gradually add the beer. Then add chile and pepper and cook over very low heat for 10 minutes, or until cheese is completely melted, stirring occasionally. Serve over toast points. Serves 4.

New Mexico Turnip Casserole

6 good-size TURNIPS,
   peeled and quartered
3 Tbsp. BUTTER
¼ tsp. NUTMEG
½ cup HEAVY CREAM

¼ tsp. ground WHITE
   PEPPER
½ lb. cooked HAM, diced
½ cup chopped GREEN
   CHILE (fresh or canned)

Cook turnips in lightly-salted water, covered, until tender. Drain and mash with butter, cream, nutmeg and pepper. Stir in ham and chile. Spoon into a lightly-buttered casserole dish. Bake in 325-degree oven for 30 minutes, or until heated through. Serves 4 to 6.

Patatas con Queso
(Potatoes with Cheese)

2 cups MASHED
POTATOES
1 cup grated CHEDDAR
CHEESE
¼ cup chopped GREEN
CHILE (fresh or canned)
¼ tsp. ground BLACK
PEPPER

¼ tsp. GARLIC SALT
1 EGG
½ cup all-purpose FLOUR
½ tsp. PAPRIKA
¼ cup COOKING OIL

Combine mashed potatoes, cheese, chile, pepper, garlic salt and form into eight equal-size patties. Beat egg. Combine flour with paprika. Dip patties in egg, first, then in flour mixture. Heat oil in a frying pan, and fry potato patties in oil until they are golden brown.   Serves 4.

Zippy Noodles

1 pkg. (12 oz.) wide
NOODLES
¼ lb. BUTTER
1 cup cooked, PEELED
TOMATOES
½ tsp. GARLIC SALT

½ tsp. ground BLACK
PEPPER
1 tsp. DRIED PARSLEY
½ cup chopped GREEN
CHILE (fresh or canned)

Cook noodles according to package directions. While noodles are cooking, melt butter in a small pan, chop tomatoes and add to pan. Add garlic salt, pepper, parsley and green chile.

Cook until noodles are done. Drain and put into a serving bowl. Pour tomato mixture over noodles and toss lightly.

                               Serves 6.

Marquezotes

This cake was served at fashionable Spanish weddings in the 18th and 19th centuries in Albuquerque.

10 EGGS, separated
1 cup SUGAR
1 tsp. VANILLA

1 cup CAKE FLOUR
½ tsp. SALT
1 tsp. BAKING POWDER

Beat egg whites until stiff. Beat egg yolks separately. Gradually add sugar and vanilla to the egg yolks. Sift flour, salt and baking powder, and add to the sugar, egg yolk mixture. Fold in egg whites and pour into a 10″ lightly buttered springform pan. Bake in 350-degree over for 45 minutes, or until tested done.

Serves 8 to 10.

Christmas Oranges Deluxe

8 large ORANGES
1 qt. French vanilla
 ICE CREAM

¼ cup GRAND MARNIER
1 tsp. ground CINNAMON

Cut a very thin slice from the base of each orange so that orange will stand upright. Then cut off upper third of each orange and scoop out orange pulp. Remove membranes. Then combine orange pulp with ice cream and Grand Marnier. Fill each orange shell and freeze. Sprinkle with cinnamon before serving. Serves 8.

Pumpkin Turnovers

16 oz. cooked, mashed
  PUMPKIN
1 cup LIGHT BROWN
  SUGAR
1 Tbsp. melted BUTTER
1 Tbsp. DARK RUM
¼ tsp. ground CLOVES

¼ tsp. ground NUTMEG
½ tsp. ground ALLSPICE
PIE CRUST DOUGH
  (enough for 2 nine-
  inch pies)
1 EGG (beaten)
SUGAR

Mix pumpkin with brown sugar, butter, rum and spices. Divide pastry into 12 portions. Roll each portion into a six-inch circle. Spoon two tablespoons of pumpkin filling on each circle, fold to form a turnover, and seal edges with the tines of a fork. Cut a vent in top to allow steam to escape while baking. Brush turnover with beaten egg and sprinkle with sugar. Bake on greased baking sheets in a 400-degree oven for 30 minutes or until nice and brown. Cool on wire racks.

Makes 12 turnovers.

Peanut Butter Biscuits

2 cups all-purpose FLOUR
2 tsp. BAKING POWDER
½ tsp. SALT

2 Tbsp. solid VEGETABLE
  SHORTENING
2 Tbsp. smooth
  PEANUT BUTTER
MILK

Sift flour, baking powder and salt together into a mixing bowl. Cut shortening into dry ingredients. Then mix peanut butter into mixture. Add just enough milk to make a soft dough. Knead on a lightly-floured pastry board or marble slab for half a minute. Pat out with your hand until about one-half-inch thick. Cut with a biscuit cutter and place biscuits on a lightly-greased baking sheet about 1½-inches apart. Bake in 450-degree oven for 15 minutes, or until golden brown.

Makes approx. one dozen.

Pinto Bean Cake

1 cup SUGAR
4 Tbsp. BUTTER
2 cups cooked PINTO
   BEANS, mashed
2 EGGS, well-beaten
1 cup all-purpose FLOUR
1 tsp. BAKING SODA
1 tsp. SALT
½ tsp. ground CLOVES
½ tsp. ground ALLSPICE
½ tsp. ground NUTMEG
1 tsp. VANILLA
2 cups peeled,
   diced APPLES
1 cup seedless RAISINS
½ cup chopped PECANS

Cream the sugar and butter together, and stir into the beans. Add the eggs. Sift the flour, baking soda and salt together and stir into the mixture. Add cloves, allspice, nutmeg and vanilla, and beat the mixture. Stir apples, raisins and pecans into the mixture. Pour into a well-buttered bundt pan and bake in a 350-degree oven for one hour (or until cake tests done). Serve with Brandied Whipped Cream.　　Serves 10 to 12.

Brandied Whipped Cream

2 cups heavy CREAM
2 Tbsp. SUGAR
1 Tbsp. BRANDY

Beat cream until it starts to stiffen. Add sugar and brandy, and continue beating until cream forms stiff peaks. Serve with Pinto Bean Cake.

CHAPTER SEVEN

Go West, Young Artist— Life in Taos!

If you are driving in Taos, along one of the narrow streets that wend their way through this quaint village, and you spot a friend driving towards you that you want to talk to—you just stop your car!

If your friend has just happened to be coming from a local establishment with a six pack, the two of you might just share it, and finish it, right there and then—in the middle of the road.

If other cars come up behind either one of your vehicles— well, they'll just have to wait until you get through with your conversation, and your beer. No one in Taos would dare blow their horn in an effort to get you to move on, so they could get by. It is just not done. It's not the custom.

Santa Fe is the "city different," but Taos is the "village unique." It is unique in that by and large, Taos is an exercise in individuality. An outsider may ask, "How does this town manage to work? What makes Taos click?"

There are no sure-fire answers to these queries. A certain evolution has obviously taken place in Taos, based on a natural Indian philosophy, reshaped by the Spanish temperament, and embraced by artists, writers and hangers-on who found a haven in Taos from the beginning of the twentieth century.

Mabel Dodge Luhan, a headstrong heiress from the east, "discovered" Taos. She made a break with the normal conventions of her time and class, married an Indian and settled in Taos. She, in turn, attracted other people from around the country.

She also begged D. H. Lawrence in letter after letter to come visit her in Taos. He finally did, complete with his wife, Frieda, and his long-time friend, The Honorable Dorothy Brett, Lady Brett.

This group lived the Bohemian life in and around Taos, sometimes writing, painting, sculpturing, often drinking and quarreling. They commanded center stage for years.

They also brought exotic foods and recipes with them and fed the "natives" on canned squid and truffles. They experimented with the local cuisine and D. H. Lawrence never missed a chance to teach someone how to make his favorite bread.

The individualism and Bohemianism that existed for many years in Taos is a romantic and enjoyable memory that many Taos residents still cherish.

"9 Sold a Painting Today!" Cocktail

Good cheer and good spirits have always been a part of the Taos lifestyle, and celebrations come easily.

**2 oz. good GIN
CHAMPAGNE**

Pour the gin over ice cubes in a large stemmed glass. Fill the glass with chilled champagne. *Salud!*   Makes 1 cocktail.

Salt-Rising Bread

D. H. Lawrence and his wife lived on a small ranch outside of Taos. The road to the ranch was not paved and was often rutted or covered with water.

Supplies were carried into the ranch by horseback and trips into town were infrequent. Therefore yeast was often in short supply. Salt-Rising Bread was a way around this shortage.

2/3 cup MILK	1 tsp. BAKING SODA
½ cup WHITE CORNMEAL	11 to 12 cups sifted all-
2 Tbsp. SUGAR	purpose FLOUR
1 Tbsp. SALT	2 cups BOILING WATER
2 cups lukewarm WATER	4 Tbsp. SHORTENING
	BUTTER (for brushing)

Scald the milk and add cornmeal, sugar and salt and beat very thoroughly. Cover with a damp tea towel and let stand overnight in a warm place.

The next morning it should be light and bubbly. If not, put the bowl in a pan of hot water and let stand until it does bubble.

Add baking soda and three cups of flour to the lukewarm water. Add cornmeal mixture and beat well. Place in a pan of hot water and keep in a warm place for an hour, or until the bubbles form again. Stir, making it go down.

Add shortening to boiling water. Let stand until it becomes lukewarm. Add flour-cornmeal mixture and mix thoroughly. Add remaining flour until it makes a stiff dough.

Knead for 10 minutes until smooth. Divide into three equal parts and form each into a ball. Cover and let stand for 10 minutes. Shape the balls into loaves and put into greased loaf pans. Brush lightly with melted shortening and let stand in a warm place for approximately two hours, or until each loaf has doubled in bulk.

Preheat oven to 400 degrees. Bake for 45 minutes, or until done, in 400-degree oven. Brush the top of each loaf with melted butter.

Makes three 1½-lb. loaves.

Fiesta Chicken Salad

4 cups diced, cooked
  CHICKEN
¾ cup coarsely-chopped
  CELERY
1 can (11 oz.) MANDARIN
  ORANGES, drained
1 can (8 oz.) PINEAPPLE
  CHUNKS, drained

1 cup CASHEWS
1 Tbsp. RED CHILE
  POWDER
¼ tsp. SALT
¼ tsp. ground WHITE
  PEPPER

Combine all ingredients in a salad bowl. Then lightly toss with the following:

> ½ pt. SOUR CREAM
> 1 cup MAYONNAISE

Chill well and serve on a bed of leaf lettuce.   Serves 8.

Taco Salad

Mabel Dodge Luhan was well known for making salads. This salad is reportedly her recipe.

1 lb. GROUND BEEF
¼ cup chopped yellow
  ONION
¼ tsp. GARLIC SALT
¼ tsp. ground BLACK
  PEPPER
2 Tbsp. chopped GREEN
  CHILE (fresh or canned)
8 oz. cooked red KIDNEY
  BEANS (or PINTO BEANS)

2 fresh, ripe TOMATOES,
  cut into wedges
12 large ripe stuffed
  OLIVES, sliced
½ cup shredded Monterey
  JACK CHEESE
¼ lb. TORTILLA CHIPS
  (or corn chips)
3 cups SALAD GREENS,
  coarsely-shredded

Cook the ground beef in a skillet with onion, spices and green chile until the beef is nicely-browned. Drain and mix with beans, tomatoes, olives, cheese and chips. Lightly toss with salad greens and serve on a bed of salad greens. Top with chips.

Serves 4.

Bean Dip

4 cups cooked PINTO BEANS
1 Tbsp. WORCESTERSHIRE SAUCE
½ tsp. CELERY SALT
1 tsp. GARLIC POWDER
1 tsp. ground CUMIN
1 tsp. ground RED CHILE POWDER
½ cup diced GREEN CHILE (fresh or canned)
1 cup Monterey JACK CHEESE, grated

Thoroughly mash the beans and place in a large pot. Stir in Worcestershire sauce, celery salt, garlic powder, cumin, red chile powder and green chile. Cook over low heat until nicely warmed through. Stir in three-fourths cup of cheese and continue cooking, stirring occasionally, until the cheese melts. Turn out mixture into a serving bowl, sprinkle remaining one-fourth cup cheese on top and serve warm with tortilla chips.

Serves 10 to 12.

Horseradish Mousse

1 cup COTTAGE CHEESE
¼ cup MILK
2 Tbsp. HORSERADISH
2 Tbsp. GARLIC VINEGAR
1 tsp. unflavored GELATIN
¼ cup COLD WATER

Whip the cottage cheese, milk, horseradish and vinegar in a blender until it is the consistency of whipped cream. Dissolve gelatin in water and stir into the cheese mixture. Pour into a mold and chill in the refrigerator at least three hours. Great as a condiment served with beef brisket.

Serves 4.

Vermicelli Soup

8 oz. VERMICELLI
2 Tbsp. BACON FAT
(or cooking oil)
1 clove GARLIC
½ small white ONION,
finely-minced
½ cup TOMATO PUREE

2 qt. CHICKEN STOCK
1 tsp. fresh PARSLEY,
chopped fine
2 tsp. ground RED CHILE
½ tsp. ground WHITE
PEPPER
½ tsp. SALT

Break up vermicelli into small pieces and saute in the fat or oil until a golden brown color. Then add garlic, onion and tomato puree, and cook for five minutes. Add stock and seasonings and cook over medium heat for 20 minutes, or until vermicelli is tender.   Serves 8.

Sopa de Vino
(Wine Soup)

2 Tbsp. BUTTER
1 med.-size yellow
ONION, finely-chopped
2 Tbsp. all-purpose
FLOUR
2 med.-size red ripe
TOMATOES, peeled
and chopped
5 cups CHICKEN STOCK

¼ tsp. GARLIC SALT
½ tsp. ground BLACK
PEPPER
1 cup DRY RED WINE
2 Tbsp. BUTTER
2 slices dry WHITE
BREAD, cubed
3 hard-cooked EGGS,
coarsely-chopped

Melt butter in a saucepan and saute onions until just golden in color. Stir in flour until smooth and a light brown. Add tomatoes and simmer for 10 minutes, covered.

Add stock and seasonings, and simmer for 15 minutes. Add wine to the mixture and cook for 10 minutes. Melt the second two tablespoons of butter and saute bread cubes for approximately five minutes over low heat until evenly browned.

Serve soup in individual bowls or mugs and garnish with chopped eggs and bread cubes.   Serves 8.

Taos Gazpacho

1 can (1 lb., No. 303) peeled ripe TOMATOES, chopppped
1 med.-size CUCUMBER, peeled and finely-chopped
1 large GREEN BELL PEPPER, seeded and finely-chopped
1 cup CELERY, finely-chopped
3 GREEN ONIONS, finely-chopped
2 cups TOMATO JUICE
2 Tbsp. DRY WHITE WINE
¼ tsp. CELERY SALT
½ tsp. ground BLACK PEPPER
½ tsp. GARLIC SALT
1 Tbsp. fresh LIME JUICE
LIME SLICES

Put chopped tomatoes with their juice in a large bowl. Add rest of ingredients (except lime slices), stir gently and chill for at least two hours before serving. Serve in soup bowls and garnish with lime slices. Serves 4 to 6.

Special-Occasion Rice

3 cups cooked RICE
½ lb. BUTTER
1 tsp. dry RED CHILE, finely-minced
¾ cup SALTED PEANUTS, finely-chopped
½ cup GREEN ONIONS, finely-chopped
1½ cups COOKED HAM, cubed
1 lb. med.-size SHRIMP
2 cloves GARLIC, chopped
½ tsp. ground BLACK PEPPER
1 tsp. dried PARSLEY

Cook rice according to package directions. Melt butter in a frying pan, stir in chile, peanuts and onions, and cook over high heat for two minutes.

Add ham and shrimp together with garlic, black pepper and parsley, and cook over medium-high heat for four to five minutes, or until shrimp are pink and done through.

Put rice into a serving dish, pour ham-and-shrimp mixture over rice and toss lightly. Serves 8.

Poached Beef Brisket

1 tsp. DRY MUSTARD
1 tsp. ground BLACK
  PEPPER
5 lbs. boneless BEEF
  BRISKET
1 med.-size yellow ONION,
  coarsely-chopped

1 stalk CELERY, with the
  leaves, coarsely-chopped
2 BAY LEAVES
1 tsp. BROWN SUGAR
2 cups COLD WATER
2 cans (12 oz. each) BEER

Rub the mustard and pepper into meat with your hands. Put all the other ingredients in the bottom of a baking pan, add meat and cover tightly with aluminum foil. Poach in 300-degree oven for 3½ to 4 hours, or until brisket is tender. Remove bay leaves before serving. Serves 8 to 10.

Green Chile Salsa

12 good-size roasted
  GREEN CHILES
1 GREEN TOMATO

½ tsp. GARLIC SALT
2 tsp. fresh CILANTRO

Peel chiles, remove stems and seeds. Peel tomato and chop in a blender. Add chile, garlic salt and cilantro to tomato and blend.   Makes approx. 1 cup.

Easy Green Bean Casserole

2 cans (16 oz. each) French-
  cut GREEN BEANS
1 can (10¾ oz.) Cream of
  MUSHROOM SOUP
½ cup SLIVERED
  ALMONDS

½ tsp. ground BLACK
  PEPPER
½ cup chopped GREEN
  CHILE (fresh or canned)
SALT to taste
BREAD CRUMBS
PAPRIKA

Drain beans and put into oven-proof baking dish. Stir in soup, almonds, pepper, chile and salt. Sprinkle bread crumbs on top, dust with paprika and bake in 350-degree oven for 30 minutes, or until heated through.   Serves 6 to 8.

Betty's Best Rice

1 med.-size WHITE ONION
2 Tbsp. BACON DRIPPINGS
3 cloves GARLIC
1½ cups uncooked
  WHITE RICE

1 cup TOMATO SAUCE
2½ cups WATER
½ cup chopped GREEN
  CHILE (fresh or canned)

Peel and finely-chop onion. Heat bacon drippings in a heavy, large frying pan or Dutch oven. Add onion. Peel and mince garlic and add. Cook until just translucent.

Then stir in rice and brown lightly. Stir in tomato sauce, water and chile. Cover and simmer over low heat for 30 minutes, or until the liquid has evaporated and rice is tender.

Serves 4 to 6.

Crispy Broiled Zucchini

2 large ZUCCHINI
⅛ lb. BUTTER
1 small white ONION
2 Tbsp. chopped GREEN
  CHILE (fresh or canned)

½ tsp. SALT
1 tsp. ground BLACK
  PEPPER
½ cup grated SWISS
  CHEESE

Wash zucchini and slice into half-inch rounds. Boil in salted water just until tender. Drain and spread zucchini in a shallow baking pan. Melt butter. Peel and grate onion and stir onion and green chile into the butter. Spread this mixture over the zucchini. Shake salt and pepper over slices. Then sprinkle cheese over it.

Broil about three inches from the heat for five minutes, or until cheese is a light brown.   Serves 4.

Sourdough Chocolate Cake

½ cup SOURDOUGH STARTER
1 cup WATER
1½ cups all-purpose FLOUR
¼ cup non-fat DRY MILK
½ cup BUTTER
1 cup SUGAR
½ tsp. SALT
1 tsp. VANILLA
1 tsp. CINNAMON
1½ tsp. BAKING SODA
2 EGGS
3 squares semi-sweet CHOCOLATE

Mix sourdough starter with water, flour and dry milk. Let this work for three hours in a warm place or until it bubbles.

Cream together butter and sugar with the eggs. Stir in salt, vanilla, cinnamon and soda. Melt chocolate and stir into sugar mixture. Then mix together with the starter. Mix at low speed until well blended.

Put into two eight-inch cake pans (or a 9x13 pan) and bake in a 350-degree oven for 30 minutes, or until the cake tests done. Turn out on a wire rack and let cool.

Frost with the following Super Easy Icing recipe.

Serves 10 to 12.

Super Easy Icing

1 cup SUGAR
1/3 cup MILK
5 Tbsp. MARGARINE
1 cup CHOCOLATE CHIPS

Combine sugar, milk and margarine in a saucepan, and bring to a boil while stirring. Boil for one minute, remove from stove, stir in chocolate chips and melt. Use to ice cake. This can also be done in your microwave.

New Mexican
New Year's Eve Hot Chocolate

2 rounds or sections of
  MEXICAN CHOCOLATE
  (Now available in most
  supermarkets)
½ cup SUGAR
1½ cups COLD WATER

1 tsp. ground NUTMEG
6 cups MILK
1 Tbsp. VANILLA
1 cup WHIPPED CREAM
GROUND CINNAMON

Combine chocolate, sugar, water and nutmeg in a pan and cook over medium heat for 10 minutes. Add milk and scald (but do not let boil), stirring constantly, until smooth. Stir in vanilla.

Divide into six heavy glasses or cups (an optional jigger of brandy may be added), then put a dollop of whipped cream on top of each glass, sprinkle with ground cinnamon and serve.

Serves 6.

CHAPTER EIGHT

The Last Frontier?

"Old Timers" the world over always have fond remembrances of the past. Many of these memories center around the food their families prepared at home, church and civic parties, and the restaurants they have frequented over the years.

As the Southwest becomes increasingly popular, and more and more people discover the appeal of the climate and the way of life—the way of life and the food naturally undergo change.

Although the Indian and Mexican influences remain strong in the way New Mexicans cook, other styles of food preparation and ethnic cultures are bringing changes and adaptations.

The influx of new residents and the impact of the media have accelerated this phenomenon. Twenty years ago quiche, endive and desserts laced with raspberry liqueur were unheard of in New Mexico. Today they are commonplace.

Although some of these new food trends, such as Shark Tacos and Green Chile Blintzes may not catch on, perhaps some future "old timers" will look back on the cuisine of today's New Mexico as "the good old days!"

Green Chile Quiche

3 Tbsp. BUTTER
2 med.-size yellow ONIONS,
  finely-chopped
1½ Tbsp. FLOUR
2 EGGS
2/3 cup WHIPPING CREAM
¼ cup TEQUILA
1 tsp. SALT
⅛ tsp. ground WHITE
  PEPPER

pinch NUTMEG
pinch PAPRIKA
pinch SAGE
¾ cup grated SWISS
  CHEESE
½ cup diced GREEN
  CHILE (fresh or canned)
9″ PIE SHELL,
  unbaked

Preheat oven to 375 degrees.

Melt butter in a frying pan and saute onions until tender and golden brown in color. Sprinkle flour over onions and cook over low heat, stirring constantly, until the onions are coated with flour. Remove from heat and let cool. Beat eggs. Beat cream, tequila, salt, pepper, nutmeg, paprika and sage into the eggs. Stir in half-cup of the cheese and chile. Pour into pie shell and sprinkle with remaining quarter-cup of cheese. Bake in 375-degree oven for 20 minutes, or until done.   Serves 6.

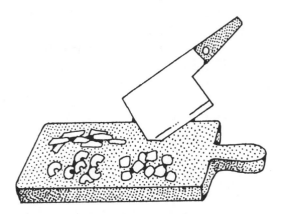

Chicken Crepes
with Green Chile Sauce

2 Tbsp. BUTTER
½ med.-size white ONION,
  finely-chopped
1 can (15 oz.) peeled
  TOMATOES, drained
  and coarsely-chopped
1 cup cooked, diced
  white meat CHICKEN

1 Tbsp. RAISINS,
  finely-chopped
½ cup ALMONDS, ground
1 Tbsp. CAPERS
6 pitted GREEN OLIVES,
  finely-chopped
5 pitted BLACK OLIVES,
  finely-chopped
8 CREPES

Melt butter in a saucepan and saute onions until soft. Add tomatoes, chicken, raisins, almonds, capers and olives.

Cook over low heat until heated thoroughly, then fill the crepes, and top with Green Chile Sauce.   Serves 4.

The Crepes

1½ cups all-purpose
  FLOUR
4 EGGS, lightly beaten
½ tsp. SALT

1½ cups MILK
⅛ lb. BUTTER
½ cup COLD WATER

Combine flour, eggs and salt in a mixing bowl. Stir in half of the milk and beat with a wire whisk until smooth. Melt butter and whisk it into mixture. Then whisk in rest of the milk and water.

Use a crepe pan or a small non-stick frying pan. Heat pan over medium heat and pour three tablespoons of batter into pan. Tilt pan back and forth until batter is spread evenly over bottom of pan. Cook for approximately one minute, then flip crepe over and cook for 30 seconds on the other side. Stack crepes on a plate and cover with a kitchen towel to keep warm until ready to use.   Yield: Approx. 8 to 12 crepes.

Green Chile Sauce

2 Tbsp. BUTTER
¼ med.-size white ONION, finely-chopped
1 med.-size GREEN BELL PEPPER, coarsely-chopped
1½ Tbsp. CORNSTARCH
1½ cups MILK

3 whole GREEN CHILES, peeled, seeded and finely-chopped
¼ cup Monterey JACK CHEESE, grated
¼ tsp. GARLIC SALT
⅛ cup DRY VERMOUTH

Melt butter in a frying pan and saute onion and pepper for five minutes. Dissolve cornstarch in milk and stir into onion-and-pepper mixture. Simmer over medium heat until mixture thickens.

Add remaining ingredients and cook over low heat until cheese dissolves. Pour over warm, stuffed crepes and bake in 400-degree oven until sauce begins to bubble and crepes are lightly browned.   Makes approx. 2 cups.

Mushrooms a la San Jose

1 lb. large, fresh
   MUSHROOMS
2 Tbsp. OLIVE OIL
¼ cup fresh LEMON JUICE
¼ tsp. SALT

½ cup chopped GREEN
   CHILE (fresh or canned)
½ tsp. fresh, minced
   GARLIC
1 cup dry WHITE WINE

Wash mushrooms well, cut off ends of stems and slice mushrooms. Mix remaining ingredients together in a saucepan and heat over low heat for five minutes. Put mushrooms in a baking dish, pour hot liquid over them, cover and bake for 30 minutes in 350-degree oven.   Serves 6.

Posole

2 Tbsp. OLIVE OIL
1 med.-size yellow ONION,
   finely-chopped
2 cloves GARLIC, run
   through a garlic press
1 lb. lean, ground PORK

1 tsp. SALT
1 tsp. dried OREGANO
2 tsps. ground CUMIN
1 cup chopped GREEN
   CHILE
1 can (#10) WHITE HOMINY,
   with the juice

Heat oil in a frying pan, saute onion and garlic until soft. Stir in ground pork, add salt, oregano, cumin and green chile, and cook until pork is brown. Pour hominy (with liquid) into a large pot, stir in pork mixture and cook, covered, over low heat for at least one hour. Serve in soup bowls with Red Chile Sauce on the side.   Serves 10 to 12.

New Year's Black-Eyed Peas

For years, the custom in many households in New Mexico has been to eat Posole on New Year's. People moving in from the South added the ritual of having ham and black-eyed peas on New Year's Day.

This is supposed to bring good luck for the year ahead to everyone who eats it. I don't know about anybody else, but I figure it's an easy way to help the fates along.

2 Tbsp. BACON DRIPPINGS
1 med.-size yellow ONION, peeled and coarsely chopped
1 clove GARLIC, peeled and minced
½ tsp. ground BLACK PEPPER
2 pkgs. fresh-frozen BLACK-EYED PEAS
WATER
SALT to taste

Melt bacon drippings in large cast-iron Dutch oven, saute onion until translucent, add garlic and pepper. Then add black-eyed peas, cover with water and simmer over low heat for 45 minutes or until the peas are tender. Then add salt to taste. (Do not add salt until the very end or it will make the skin on the peas split open.)   Serves 6.

Fajitas

juice of 2 large LIMES
2 Tbsp. OLIVE OIL
¼ cup chopped CILANTRO
1 med.-size JALAPEÑO,
  seeded and minced
2 cloves GARLIC,
  finely-minced
½ tsp. ground CUMIN
½ tsp. SALT
½ tsp. ground BLACK
  PEPPER
2 lbs. SKIRT STEAK
  or flank steak
2 med.-size AVOCADOS,
  peeled and sliced
1 med.-size yellow or white
  ONION, thinly-sliced

Mix lime juice, oil, cilantro, jalapeño, garlic, cumin, salt and pepper in a bowl. Marinate steak in this mixture, cover, for at least eight hours in the refrigerator. Remove steak and grill or broil with sliced onions to taste. Slice across the grain into one-quarter-inch-thick slices and arrange on large platter with onions and sliced avocados. Serve with warm flour tortillas and Salsa Fresca.   Serves 6.

Salsa Fresca

2 med.-size fresh
  TOMATOES, finely-
  chopped
½ med.-size white ONION,
  finely-chopped
6 GREEN ONIONS,
  finely-chopped
2 Tbsp. fresh CILANTRO,
  finely-chopped
2 JALAPEÑOS, seeded and
  finely-chopped
1/3 cup LIME JUICE
1 oz. white TEQUILA

Mix all ingredients and refrigerate at least two hours before serving.   Approx. 1 cup.

Easy
Barbecued Short Ribs

1 yellow ONION
2 Tbsp. BACON
    DRIPPINGS
3 lbs. beef SHORT RIBS
¼ cup RED WINE VINEGAR
2 Tbsp. light BROWN
    SUGAR
1 cup chopped GREEN
    CHILE

½ cup diced CELERY
½ cup TOMATO SAUCE
½ cup WATER
3 Tbsp. WORCESTERSHIRE
    SAUCE
1 Tbsp. prepared
    YELLOW MUSTARD
2 tsp. SALT
1 tsp. GARLIC POWDER

Finely chop onion. Melt drippings in a large Dutch oven or pan and brown onion for five minutes. Add short ribs and brown. Sitr in remaining ingredients, cover and cook over low heat for two hours, or until done.   Serves 6 to 8.

Barbecued Brisket

1 beef BRISKET (8 to 10 lbs.)	1 cup WATER
1 cup dry WHITE WINE	2 Tbsp. dried minced ONIONS

Put brisket in a baking pan with wine, water and onions. Cover with tin foil and bake in 250-degree oven overnight (10 to 12 hours), or until meat is tender. Let meat stand while you make the following sauce. (The meat is easier to slice when slightly cooled.)

1 btl. (14 oz.) KETCHUP®	2 cloves GARLIC, run through a garlic press
¾ cup light BROWN SUGAR	
½ cup RED WINE VINEGAR	1 tsp. ground BLACK PEPPER
1½ cups WATER	
½ cup LEMON JUICE	½ cup chopped GREEN CHILE
¼ cup prepared MUSTARD	
2 Tbsp. WORCESTERSHIRE SAUCE	TABASCO® to taste
	1 med.-size yellow ONION, minced
1 Tbsp. light SOY SAUCE	
	1 Tbsp. CILANTRO

Mix all ingredients together in a saucepan and simmer over medium heat for 30 minutes.

Slice brisket, pour sauce over slices and heat in 325-degree oven for 30 minutes. Serves 12 to 15.

Barbecued Chicken

2 CHICKENS (2 to 2½ lbs. each)

Split chickens in half lengthwise and break joints of hips, wings and drumsticks so they will stay flat during cooking. Wash and pat dry.

¼ lb. BUTTER	½ cup LEMON JUICE
4 Tbsp. HEINZ 57 SAUCE®	4 Tbsp. tarragon VINEGAR
2 Tbsp. prepared MUSTARD	1 Tbsp. ground RED CHILE

Melt butter and mix with rest of ingredients. Put chicken on an open grill and brush frequently with sauce until it is all used up. Cook chicken until done through or about 45 minutes.

Serves 4.

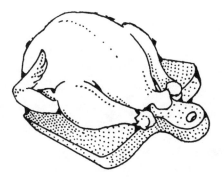

TIP: *To increase the amount of juice you get from a lemon or lime put it in the microwave on high for 15 to 30 seconds, and then let cool before juicing. DO NOT leave it any longer than 30 seconds or it might explode.*

30-Minute Hunter's Steak

2 lbs. STEAK
  (1" thick, well-marbled)
  cut into bite-size pieces
½ tsp. ground BLACK
  PEPPER
1 tsp. PAPRIKA
¼ cup BUTTER
  (or margarine)

1 cup fresh, sliced
  MUSHROOMS
¼ med.-size YELLOW
  ONION, chopped
½ cup chopped GREEN
  CHILE (fresh or canned)
2/3 cup dry RED WINE
1 cup SOUR CREAM
SALT to taste

Sprinkle steak pieces with pepper and paprika. Heat butter (or margarine) in a large skillet and brown meat on both sides. Remove meat, put mushrooms and onions in pan, and saute for 15 minutes. Stir in chile.

Add more butter or margarine, if necessary. Return the steak to the pan. Add the wine and cook, covered, over low heat for 30 minutes. Stir in sour cream and let simmer for 10 minutes more or until done. Serve on noodles or rice.

Serves 4 to 6.

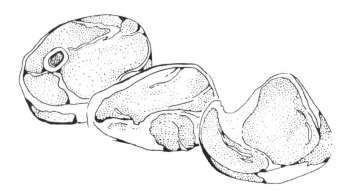

Favorite Pork Roast

I have been making this and variations of it for many years. The pork industry advertises pork as "white" meat. No matter what its color, this roast certainly tastes great.

½ tsp. ground WHITE
   PEPPER
1 tsp. ROSEMARY
1 boneless, rolled
   PORK ROAST (3½ lbs.)
1 APPLE

1 PEAR
1 cup MANDARIN
   ORANGES
1 cup dry WHITE WINE
1 cup LUKEWARM WATER

Rub pepper and rosemary into the roast and place in a roasting pan. Core and slice apple and pear, and add to the pan. Add oranges and wine mixed with water. Bake in 325-degree oven for 2 to 2½ hours, or until done, basting with liquid several times. Remove, let cool slightly, slice and serve.

Serves 4 to 6.

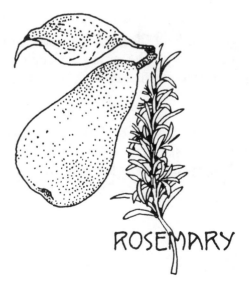

ROSEMARY

Crustless Zucchini Pizza

This recipe is great for diet-conscious pizza lovers.

2 cups grated raw
ZUCCHINI
1 tsp. SALT
1 large clove GARLIC,
minced
1 med.-size yellow ONION,
chopped fine
1 med. GREEN BELL
PEPPER, diced
½ lb. fresh MUSHROOMS,
sliced
2 Tbsp. OLIVE OIL

1 can (16 oz.)
TOMATO PASTE
½ cup chopped GREEN
CHILE (fresh or canned)
2 EGGS, well-beaten
½ tsp. chopped fresh BASIL
½ tsp. dried OREGANO
12 oz. MOZZARELLA
CHEESE
¼ cup grated PARMESAN
CHEESE
2 Tbsp. FLOUR

Put zucchini in a strainer, sprinkle with salt. Let stand for 45 minutes, then rinse with cold water. Drain well and set aside. Meanwhile, mix garlic, onion, bell pepper, mushrooms and oil in a frying pan. Saute until tender. Strain vegetables, discard liquid. Mix vegetables with tomato paste and green chile. Set aside.

Heat broiler. Lightly grease 10-inch pie pan. Mix together eggs, basil, oregano and half of mozzarella, half of parmesan and the flour. Combine with the strained zucchini in a bowl. Pour into prepared pan. Pat it out with your hands until it covers the pan. Put under broiler for 10 minutes until it is golden brown.

Put in 350-degree oven, spread on tomato paste mixture and top with remaining cheeses. Bake 10 to 20 minutes, or until golden brown. Cool on wire rack for five to 10 minutes and serve.   Serves 6 to 8.

Fried Cantaloupe

Cantaloupes are plentiful in New Mexico in the summer. This is a different way of enjoying this excellent fruit.

1 large ripe CANTALOUPE
4 Tbsp. powdered SUGAR
¼ cup white CREME
    DE MENTHE
¼ cup all-purpose FLOUR

1 cup SWEET
    DESSERT WINE
2 Tbsp. melted BUTTER
1 EGG WHITE
OIL for deep frying

Quarter the melon, peel, remove seeds and slice each quarter lengthwise into four thin wedges. Put into a bowl. Sprinkle sugar over cantaloupe wedges, pour creme de menthe over them, stir and chill in refrigerator for at least two hours.

Mix together flour, wine and butter, and beat until smooth. Beat egg white and fold into flour mixture. Dip cantaloupe wedges into batter. Heat oil in a deep-fat fryer. Put melon wedges into a basket and fry until golden brown. Drain on paper towels and serve.   Serves 4.

French 75 Peaches

4 med.-size PEACHES
4 SUGAR CUBES
ANGOSTURA® BITTERS

4 tsp. BRANDY
Split of CHAMPAGNE

Peel, pit and halve peaches. Drop one sugar cube in each of four large champagne or dessert dishes. Shake a couple of dashes of bitters on each cube, pour a teaspoon of brandy over cubes and stir well. Add two peach halves to each glass and coat with the brandy mixture. Refrigerate for at least an hour.

When ready to serve, pour equal amount of chilled champagne over peaches and serve.   Serves 4.

Mango Cobbler

2 cans (#303) MANGOES
2 tsp. APPLE PIE SPICE
2 Tbsp. BISQUICK®
  plus 2½ cups BISQUICK®

½ cup HALF & HALF
1 Tbsp. liquid SUGAR
  SUBSTITUTE
3 Tbsp. melted BUTTER

Combine mangoes and apple pie spice in a saucepan with juice. Heat over low heat. Gently stir two tablespoons of Bisquick® into mangoes to thicken sauce. Pour into the bottom of a 9 x 13″ Pyrex® baking dish.

Mix together the 2½ cups Bisquick®, half and half, sugar substitute and butter to form a dough. Drop by tablespoons onto the top of mango mixture. Bake in 425-degree oven for 30 minutes, or until done.
        Serves 8.

Pecan Turtles

2 cups FLOUR
1½ cups BROWN SUGAR
½ cup soft MARGARINE
2/3 cup BUTTER

1 cup PECAN HALVES
1 pkg. (6 oz.) CHOCOLATE
CHIPS

Mix flour, one cup of brown sugar and margarine together to form a crust and press into an ungreased 13 x 9-inch pan. Melt butter, mix with remaining half-cup of brown sugar and pour over pecans which have been layered on the crust. Bake approximately 20 minutes until it bubbles in preheated 350-degree oven.

Sprinkle chocolate chips over all, allow them to melt and then spread to cover. Cool and cut into squares.

Makes approx. 24 squares.

Chocolate Pecan Ice Cream

3 oz. UNSWEETENED
CHOCOLATE
3 EGG YOLKS
1 cup EVAPORATED MILK
2 cups HEAVY CREAM

ARTIFICIAL SWEETENER
to taste
1 tsp. VANILLA
½ cup chopped PECANS

Melt chocolate (easy way to do this is in the microwave). Let chocolate cool. While it is cooling, beat egg yolks, and then beat in the evaporated milk and cream.

When chocolate is cool, add it to the mixture. Stir in sweetener, vanilla and pecans, and freeze in an ice cream maker.

Makes approx. 1 quart.

TIP: *If you place unshelled pecans in a saucepan, cover with cold water and heat until the water just comes to a boil—then let cool—they will shell easier and the nuts will have a tendency to come out in perfect halves.*

Tequila Sherbet

1 ½ cups SUGAR
3 cups WATER
½ tsp. grated LIME PEEL
½ cup LIME JUICE

1/3 cup white TEQUILA
1 EGG WHITE
¼ tsp. COARSE SALT

Combine sugar and water in a saucepan, bring to a boil and cook for approximately five minutes. Stir in lime peel and lime juice, remove from heat and pour into a freezer tray. Freeze until mixture is thick but not completely frozen.

Remove mixture and place in blender. Add tequila, egg whites and salt, and blend thoroughly. Put mixture back into freezer tray and freeze until firm. Serve in individual dessert dishes with a twist of lime peel for garnish.   Serves 4 to 6.

Graham Cracker Crust

1½ cups GRAHAM
   CRACKER CRUMBS
4 Tbsp. SUGAR

½ cup BUTTER
   (or margarine), melted

Mix all ingredients together. Lightly butter an 8-inch pie pan. Press the graham cracker mixture on the bottom and sides of the pie pan with your hands, making sure it is even.

Pie Crust

2 cups all-purpose FLOUR,
   sifted
1 tsp. SALT

2/3 cup vegetable
   SHORTENING
6 Tbsp. COLD WATER

Sift flour and salt into a mixing bowl, and cut in shortening with a fork or pastry cutter. Gently stir in cold water. Lightly flour a marble slab or pastry board. Divide the dough in half and roll out to fit the pie pans.

Yield: Two 9-inch pie crusts

NOTES: To make one 9-inch pie crust—exactly halve the ingredients.

Or, make the two crusts, divide in half and put the half you are not going to use in a plastic bag and freeze.

TIP: *I find that two things will make a pie crust fail: if it is overworked—or gets too hot. If you find that your hands get too hot when working with the pie crust, dip them in ice water before continuing.*

Recipe Index

Photograph by Cheryl Thornburg

*Meet
the
Author*

Lynn Nusom has owned and operated award winning restaurants and was the executive chef of a four-star four-diamond hotel. He writes a syndicated newspaper column on food, reviews cookbooks, writes magazine articles on cooking and makes frequent appearances on television demonstrating cooking techniques.

Lynn Nusom is the author of seven books; *Cooking in the Land of Enchantment, The Tequila Cookbook, Spoon Deserts; Custards, Cremes and Elegant Fruit Desserts, Christmas in Arizona, The Billy the Kid Cookbook, Christmas in New Mexico,* and the *New Mexico Cook Book.*

The author and his wife, Guylyn, a native New Mexican, make their home in southern New Mexico.

ORDER BLANK

GOLDEN WEST PUBLISHERS

☼ 4113 N. Longview Ave. • Phoenix, AZ 85014

602-265-4392 • **1-800-658-5830** • FAX 602-279-6901

Qty	Title	Price	Amount
	Apple-Lovers' Cook Book	6.95	
	Arizona Cook Book	5.95	
	Best Barbecue Recipes	5.95	
	Chili-Lovers' Cook Book	5.95	
	Christmas in Arizona Cook Book	8.95	
	Christmas in New Mexico Cook Book	8.95	
	Colorado Favorites Cook Book	5.95	
	Cowboy Cartoon Cook Book	5.95	
	Easy Recipes for Wild Game & Fish	6.95	
	Favorite Pumpkin Recipes	6.95	
	Joy of Muffins	5.95	
	Mexican Desserts & Drinks	6.95	
	New Mexico Cook Book	5.95	
	Pecan-Lovers' Cook Book	6.95	
	Quick-n-Easy Mexican Recipes	5.95	
	Recipes for a Healthy Lifestyle	6.95	
	Salsa Lovers Cook Book	5.95	
	Sedona Cook Book	7.95	
	Tequila Cook Book, The	7.95	
	Texas Cook Book	5.95	
Add $2.00 to total order for shipping & handling			$2.00

☐ My Check or Money Order Enclosed. . . . . $_____

☐ MasterCard   ☐ VISA

Acct. No.   Exp. Date

Signature

Name   Telephone

Address

City/State/Zip

Call for FREE catalog

9/94   MasterCard and VISA Orders Accepted ($20 Minimum)

New Mex.

This order blank may be photo-copied.